HOLY FAMILIES

Holy Families
shadows of the trinity

MEGAN MCKENNA

VERITAS

In gratitude for all mothers and fathers in our families born of the Trinity: Father, Child and Spirit, and for those given to us to be family and friends of God: Joseph, Mark, David, Catherine and Les; and to all those who have gone before us in faith, especially Francis and Marguerite, Harold, Norene and Mimi.

Published 2018 by
Veritas Publications
7–8 Lower Abbey Street
Dublin 1
Ireland
publications@veritas.ie
www.veritas.ie

ISBN 978 1 84730 805 4

10 9 8 7 6 5 4 3 2 1

Cover designed by Barbara Croatto, Veritas
Printed in Ireland by KC Print, Kerry

Veritas books are printed on paper made from the wood pulp of managed forests. For every tree felled, at least one tree is planted, thereby renewing natural resources.

Contents

Introduction

'In the name of the Father, and of the Son, and of the Holy Spirit.' These familiar words begin practically all of our prayers. We sign ourselves lengthwise, crossing and encompassing all that is above and below, and then reaching out, stretching to include all that exists around us. We, in our bodies, are formed in this sign of the cross, in the blessing of The Three who are One, the Trinity that is the mystery of our God with us. We take this formation, this blessing for granted, often unawares of its inclusion and communion, and all that it reveals about the nature of the universe, of us and of God. Thomas Merton wrote: 'We are already one. But we imagine we are not. And what we have to recover is our original unity. What we have to be is what we already are.'[1]

This image of the Trinity, with its threeness and its oneness, forms much of the basic symbolism of practically everything we know and believe. This book seeks to look at the foundation of human life – the family – within this symbol as revelatory of God. Using the words of the theologian Leonardo Boff:

> Within this coherence and symphony I dare to assert that the whole Trinity has communicated itself, revealed itself, and definitely entered into our history. The Divine Family, in a specific moment of evolution, took the form of a human family. The Father personalised himself in Joseph, the Son in Jesus, and the Holy Spirit in Mary. It is as if the whole universe prepared the conditions for this event of infinite goodness.[2]

In the recent Post-Synodal Apostolic Exhortation *Amoris Laetitia*, this concept of the human family and the original Holy Family of Joseph, Jesus and Mary is seen in this light of the Holy Family the Trinity. It is simply and forthrightly stated:

1 *The Asian Journal of Thomas Merton* (New York: New Directions, 1973), p. 308.
2 *Saint Joseph: The Father of Jesus in a Fatherless Society*, trans. Alexandre Guilherme (Eugene, Oregon: Cascade Books, 2009), pp. 9–10.

Scripture and Tradition give us access to a knowledge of the Trinity, which is revealed with the features of a family. The family is the image of God, who is a communion of persons. At Christ's Baptism, the Father's voice was heard, calling Jesus his beloved Son, and in this love we can recognise the Holy Spirit (cf. MK 1:10-11).[3]

And in the first pages of the document, it states:

> The triune God is a communion of love, and the family is its living reflection. Saint John Paul II shed light on this when he said, 'Our God in his deepest mystery is not solitude, but a family, for he has within himself fatherhood, sonship and the essence of the family, which is love. That love, in the divine family, is the Holy Spirit.' The family is thus not unrelated to God's very being.[4]

In this book we consider Joseph, Jesus and Mary as shadows of the Father, the Son and the Spirit in the Trinity, and subsequently all human families of fathers, children and mothers as shadows of the persons in the Trinity. The Family of the Trinity is holy, and because of the Trinity, Incarnation, Resurrection and the Giving of the Spirit, all families are holy.

The word 'shadow' was carefully chosen for the title because of its theological traditions and because of its varied commonplace meanings in contemporary usage. Here are a few of the more pertinent ones:

> SHADOW *n.* 1. shade. 2. a patch of this with the shape of the body that is blocking the rays. 3. a person's inseparable attendant or companion. 4. a slight trace. 5. a shaded part of a picture. 6. gloom. 7. something weak or insubstantial.
> *v.* 1. to cast shadow over. 2. to follow and watch secretly.

---

3 *Amoris Laetitia* (AL) of the Holy Father Francis to Bishops, Priests and Deacons, Consecrated Persons, Christian Married Couples and all the Lay Faithful: On Love in the Family (2016), 71, quoting *Relatio Finalis* (2015), 38.

4 Ibid., 11, quoting *Homily at the Eucharistic Celebration in Puebla de los Angeles* (28 January 1979), 2: AAS, 71 (1979), 184.

> You, eternal Trinity, are a deep sea.
> Catherine of Siena

Stand on a shore in the darkest part of the night, just before dawn, and wait and watch for the sun to rise. Everything is in deep darkness: the sand, the sky, the waters. One can barely discern where one begins and ends. The sun slowly inches its way up and casts shadows across the water, the sand and everything present, including those who wait and watch. The shadows lengthen until all is bathed in sunlight.

Throughout the rest of the day your shadow issues from your reality, hiding or revealing where the sun spreads, lengthening and shortening until it seems to disappear inside you once again. Our shadow is always with us, a silent companion, an inseparable attendant. It carries overtones of a vast range of depth and shallowness; length, distortion; a sense of fear or something to play with, as children playing 'Me and my shadow'. There are innumerable ways of looking at and realising connections to the body that casts it or hides it.

The word 'shadow', in Spanish *ombre*, has a long theological history. It is often translated or expressed as 'overshadow', 'cloud', 'tabernacle', 'tent' and 'dwelling'. It is based on the belief that all human beings are created in the image and likeness of God. We often speak of God having eyes, hands, feet, mouth, even though we also believe that God is pure Spirit (until God becomes flesh in the person of Jesus in the family of Joseph and Mary). The Jewish scholars explain some of what is understood by us being shadows of God:

> Whenever we cast a shadow, our body forms a likeness of itself. The shadow is not our body. It may or may not have the precise shape of our body. Yet it is cast from our body. As we move, the shadow changes. In the same way, as we follow God's commandments, we cast a shadow of God's likeness.
>
> If we do good, we form God's right hand. If we resist evil, we form God's left hand. By turning away from evil, we form God's eye. By denying falsehood, we form God's ears. If we walk in the way of the Torah, we form the feet of God. We are not only created in the image of God, we also cast God's image with our actions, with our thoughts,

with our very breath. One who loves God casts a giant shadow that embraces all worlds.[5]

In our Judeo-Christian tradition, we often use this image when talking about the Spirit. In the Greek text of Luke we find that 'the Spirit will put his tent over' Mary (Lk 1:35). Many translations read that 'the Spirit will overshadow her' or 'the power of the Most High will overshadow you'. The Spirit gives birth to the Child in her before she gives birth to Jesus in her flesh.

In Hebrew there isn't really a word that can be translated as 'to dwell', as one suggestion of the Spanish expression of 'shadow' would have it. Our ancestors were nomads travelling and seeking a home. One of the ways they spoke about where and how they lived was to 'put the tent up' (*sakan*). This root word is also closely tied to the word *shekinah*, which is the presence of God that travelled with the people and 'radiated from his tent'. The word for tent is *skene*.

Another word closely aligned is 'cloud'. Clouds too cast shadows! It is said that this is the background for all that happens in the first forty chapters of the Book of Exodus. The way the Holy One travels with them is a 'cloud by day and fire by night', or as Boff writes, the cloud, the tent or dwelling place of God casts a shadow revealing the presence of God.

[This image] symbolises the maternal and protective presence of God, a presence that reveals itself by hiding and that is hidden by revealing itself. The cloud accompanies the Jewish people in their wanderings around the desert. When the cloud moved, they wandered, when the cloud did not move, then they remained where they were. In fact, the cloud is a symbol for the mysterious character of the presence of God, something that we see but that we cannot touch and which is something luminous and dark, something that appears and vanishes, something that fascinates and strikes fear at the same time (cf. Exod 14:20). Both the cloud and the tent cast a shadow. The shadow can be seen but it cannot be touched. Shadow and cloud reveal by concealing and conceal by revealing the indescribable presence of God.

---

5   Jiří Langer, *Nine Gates* (Cambridge: Lutterworth Press, 1987), pp. 170–1.

The following reasoning is reached at this point: by putting up their tent amongst us, as the Holy Spirit did to Mary (cf. Lk 1:35) or the Word to Jesus (cf. Jn 1:14), these divine Persons started to permanently dwell among us. Their dwelling stands for a real and live presence, however mysterious and indescribably it is, which is suggested by the symbolism of the cloud and the shadow.[6]

So, this book is filled with shadows! The first is the Spirit of God that was often referred to among the early Christians as 'the shadow of Jesus bent over the lives of his friends'. This shadow is the first gift all of us receive in the Body of Christ at Baptism and the first gift given to the Church after Jesus' Resurrection and Ascension. Because of the Incarnation, there is no place where God is not – the shadow is everywhere. The Trinity itself casts its shadow individually – Father, Child, the flesh of the Father and the Spirit – and together they are Family in communion. And in the human family of Jesus, the shadow of the Father is cast upon Joseph (overshadows him), the shadow of the Spirit overshadows Mary, and the shadow of Jesus is cast within and over every one of us. The shadow of the Trinity is cast by every family. Therefore, every family, like Jesus' own family, is holy, is the dwelling place where God abides with us, is revealed to us and through us, is how God's presence is known, felt and experienced in our lives and world.

The history of the family from the beginning of time and from our beginnings as Judeo-Christians in the book of Genesis is our primary relationship that leads to an understanding of ourselves as persons and in society. It is also at the heart of the gift of the growing understanding of the Jewish people's relationship with God. God is the parent of Israel, both protective father and nurturing mother. The people of Israel are the sons and daughters, the children of God. Israel is also the wife of God (see the books of Wisdom and the writings of the prophets). Israel is to listen and to obey God. They are bound in covenant, a marriage of mutual love and intimacy. As close as the one flesh that husband and wife are to become is the image for the oneness of spirit that is to be between God and Israel.

---

6   Boff, *Saint Joseph*, op. cit., pp. 105–6. For further extrapolation of this idea, see all of Chapter 7 of Boff's work, entitled 'Saint Joseph of God: The Order of Hypostatic Union' (pp. 97–110).

However, it helps us to remember that this history envisioning such closeness, faithfulness and intimacy is also a ragged history of separation, unfaithfulness and betrayal. More often than not there is as much failure in the experience of the dream as there is hope in the vision that they and we are called to live and reveal to others. This reality of failure is present in the people as a whole over history and in individuals. The hope of what a marriage is and what a family can become is like a mirror with many cracks, break points, scratches and ragged pieces left of what was to clearly speak of God's dwelling within us and among us. The earlier Testament, the New Testament and the two thousand years that have passed since Jesus' return to the Father, while remaining with us in his Risen Spirit, also reads as a sad epic of the dream yet to become reality. Regarding families and marriage, husband and wife, parent and child, the stories range from shocking, discouraging, fraught with darkness, disowning and disavowing of connections, seeping jealousy, intrigue, lies, colluding with evil, abusing power, refusing to even acknowledge familiar ties. And it stretches to include outsiders, enemies and people from every caste and country.

A friend theologian calls this the history of 'the unholy family' and says it cannot be ignored. There is a terribly strong ambiguity both in the relationship that God has with Israel and in all human families. This continues even in the New Testament, in Jesus' own family situation and in the family situations of those around him in society. There are unholy elements in Jesus' family in Mark's Gospel that begins with Jesus as an adult who preaches God's Good News to the poor and almost immediately is met with opposition, hostility and rejection. Here is the first time we meet Jesus in relation to his family and they are not among his disciples. 'When his family heard it, they went out to seize him, for people were saying, "He has gone out of his mind"' (Mk 3:21). Later, when Jesus is in Nazareth, we read that Jesus 'could do no mighty work there' (Mk 6:5). The people think they know his family of origins and 'they took offence at him' (Mk 6:3).

There is a story narrated in Mark, Matthew and Luke that describes this 'unholy' reality of Jesus' family, of all our families. We have to look at it honestly and integrate it into our understanding of being Christians and finding ourselves in our own families and in the family of God.

> Then his mother and his brothers came; and standing outside, they sent to him and called him. A crowd was sitting around him; and they said to him, 'Your mother and your brothers and sisters are outside, asking for you.' He replied, 'Who are my mother and my brothers?' And looking at those who sat around him, he said, 'Here are my mother and my brothers! Whoever does the will of God is my brother and sister and mother.' (Mk 3:31-35)[7]

Our family of origin is just that, the family of our beginnings. As believers, as Christians, our family must expand and become deeper to include many others, eventually to include the entire human family, as we obey and seek to render the Family of the Trinity in our lives. We are born into this family and grow in wisdom, age and grace in this family as we 'do the will of God'. In Luke's version, those who are Jesus' new family by water and by the Spirit 'hear the word of God and do it'. We should not be surprised that these same tensions, pressures and oppositions lie in our own families too. Our family of origin is where we begin, our first stepping stone on the path to living in an ever-widening circle that includes more and more mothers and fathers, brothers and sisters, blood kin and those bound to us by our God. God calls us to the vocation of living as beloved children of God, with Jesus, bound in his strong nurturing Spirit to our Father, who carries us all in his arms. Our essential vocation is to live in God, the Trinity.

The Gospels in many ways give us hope. The sense of Jesus' own family goes from one extreme to the other: the shadows are both ominous and grace-filled. As in the stories since our beginnings in Genesis up until today, families, the marriage relationship, the relationship with parents and children and the place of family in the rest of society are both problematic and hopeful. The stories taken together provide us with a basic reality – the shadows of the Trinity as family and the reality that each person, each couple, each family struggles to make the vision come true in their lives and situations. All fail in many small, repetitive ways, sometimes disastrous ones, and all have moments of glory and delight. Most often the resemblance can be described as a cloud, a shadow that both reveals and conceals with depth, light and shallowness and distortion.

---

7 Cf. also Mt 12:46-50 and Lk 8:19-21.

The closing paragraph of the paper 'A Holy Family?' summarises it thusly:

> Nazareth and Bethlehem, rootlessness, newness and continuity, family as opponents and family as disciples … these opposites, with all the tensions they imply, are necessary in order to confront and come to know more deeply the surprising fulfilment of the promises of God in Jesus son of Mary (and Joseph too).[8]

We will look at the basic underlying reality of family. Then we will look at Mary as the Spirit's shadow, the Child as Light, Joseph as the shadow of the Father, Joseph and Mary as husband and wife and parents, children as those who are growing up to be disciples of Jesus and our becoming more and more integral and intimate with the family of the world as we move deeper into the Trinity. We move from one family to another, believing there is only one Holy Family of the Trinity, being drawn into Love and our true identity at the last.

---

8   David M. Neuhaus, SJ, 'A Holy Family? A Biblical meditation on Jesus' family in the Synoptic Gospels', in M. Ferrero and R. Spataro (eds), *Tuo padre e io ti cercavamo: Studi in onore de Don Joan Maria Vernet* (Jerusalem: Studium Theologicum Salesianum, 2007), pp. 33–55.

Chapter 1
The Family

The family is the nucleus of civilization.
Will Durant

Call it a clan, call it a network, call it a tribe, call it a family.
Whatever you call it, whoever you are, you need one.
Jane Howard

Generally speaking, we all find our beginnings in our 'family of origin'. These families are part of the universal family of humankind, a universal community where we are all one at our roots, living on this one planet, in a shared, vast and still unknown universe. These families of origin basically consist of a father, a mother and a child or children. The father's gift: semen; the mother's gift: an ovum, a womb; and the child to be born the result of the sexual merging of the two, biologically and physically the emergence of another human being. This is the essence of family. But families diverge into myriad forms from this moment forward. And fathers and mothers are not necessarily made in that initial convergence. Families and their members, husband/fathers, wives/mothers and children, all become and evolve through experiences that are dependent on culture, race, economics, nationality, psychological backgrounds, hereditary genes, history, geography and religion. So we begin with these statements to situate families within our belief, our hope and our God who is a family: The Trinity of the Father, the Child and the Spirit/Mother. And since we are made in the image and likeness of our God, all families are holy. Every father is a shadow of the Father. Every mother is a shadow of the Spirit and every child is a shadow of the Child Jesus, the First Born of all creation. Every family is a shadow of the Trinity.

In the early Church, as mentioned in the introduction, the Spirit of God was described as 'The shadow of Jesus bent over the lives of his friends'. With the Incarnation – the foundational mystery of our God becoming flesh and blood, bone, body and soul, a human dwelling among us – this image of God takes on all the characteristics, limitations and wild possibilities of grace that we in turn reflect, image and shadow in our own lives and persons. In the second chapter of *Amoris Letitia*, Pope Francis writes:

> Faithful to Christ's teaching we look to the reality of the family today in all its complexity, with both its lights and shadows … Anthropological and cultural change in our time influence all aspects of life and call for an analytic and diversified approach.[1]

In a sense each of us becomes an icon that is a glimpse, a doorway or a window into the reflection of God, whose shadow is now found in strong ways in every man, every woman and every child from when they are conceived until they know death. All of life is revelatory, providing images and shadows, traces of who our God is among us, and in all of us everywhere, all the time. We often think of shadows as possessing purely negative connotations, but they are the areas where the deepest and broadest transformations occur. They are the potential points of conversion and hope for the future. Each of us looks like God. Every family looks like the Trinity. As God is holy, every family is holy. Early in *Amoris Laetitia*, we find this defining statement:

> The triune God is a communion of love, and the family is its living reflection. Saint John Paul II shed light on this when he said, 'Our God in his deepest mystery is not solitude, but a family, for he has within himself fatherhood, sonship and the essence of the family, which is love. That love, in the divine family, is the Holy Spirit. The family is thus not unrelated to God's very being.'[2]

Within the last fifty or so years, the family unit was often referred to as a nuclear family, meaning it was comprised of a mother, a father and child or children. However this is a misleading image. The word 'nuclear' has so many destructive, violent, exclusive and terrifying connections, with nuclear weapons, nuclear power, nuclear leaks and explosions.

---

1 AL, 32, quoting *Relatio Synodi* (2014), 5.
2 Ibid., 9–10, quoting *Homily at the Eucharistic Celebration in Puebla de los Angeles* (28 January 1979), 2: AAS 71 (1979), 184.

And throughout the world, this limited description no longer reveals the actual reality of families as they are lived and experienced. Prior to this definition, families were often called traditional families based on the original configuration, but from time immemorial that also meant extended families including a wide range of kinship relations: ancestors, grandparents, aunts, uncles, in-laws, sisters, brothers, cousins and those incorporated into all these units by marriage, adoption, necessity, circumstances or even friendship.

In the opening chapter of *Amoris Laetitia*, we are reminded that:

> The Bible is full of families, births, love stories and family crisis. This is true from its very first page, with the appearance of Adam and Eve's family with all its burden of violence but also its enduring strength (cf. Gn 4) to its very last page, where we behold the wedding feast of the Bride and the Lamb (Rv 21:2, 9). Jesus' description of the two houses, one built on rock and the other on sand (cf. Mt 7:24-27), symbolises any number of family situations shaped by the exercise of their members' freedom, for, as the poet says, 'every home is a lampstand.'[3]

Today these extended families include many groups that are referred to as blended families, single-parent families, gay and lesbian families, adopted families – those created by members who chose their children and/or parents and many who are absorbed into existing families or relationships because of the loss of one parent or both from sickness, violence, abandonment, war, rape, migration and political and economic circumstances. All families are holy. All families are shadows of our God who is family, the Holy Trinity. As Archbishop Desmond Tutu put it on the occasion of his enthronement as Anglican Archbishop of Cape Town in 1966, 'You don't choose your family. They are God's gift to you, as you are to them.' We must keep returning to this reality, this mystery and this invitation to become holy together in the basic relationships and experiences of our lives, no matter our religion nor our place in society.

The institution of marriage in society has radically changed, evolved and developed over the last fifty years. Marriage rates are declining in

---

3   Ibid., 8, quoting Jorge Luis Borges, 'Calle Desconocida', from his *Fervor de Buenos Aires* (1923; 2011), p. 23.

many western and first world countries. Recent statistics in the United States posit that 55 per cent of parents between the ages of 28–34 were not married when they had their first child. Studies show that those living outside of marriage with children are low income families and households. About 46 per cent of those living in poverty had a child before marriage.

The 2016 Canadian Census data on families, households and marital status reveals a cultural shift that affects all areas of life. According to Andrea Mrozek and Peter Jon Mitchel:

> In 2001 married couples made up 84 per cent of all couples. Today the number is 78.7 per cent. As marriage has declined, more couples choose to live together outside of marriage. 'Shacking up,' as it was once known, described the living arrangements of 16.4 per cent of all couples in 2001. That has risen to 21 per cent of all couples today.[4]

Today single parenting and cohabitating without marriage contributes to the rising divorce rates in many countries, as well as being tied to rising poverty. This trend – between rising divorce rates and poverty and cohabitation within the reality of institutional marriage – is reflected as well in sacramental marriages in many countries. In another article in *Praire Messenger*, we find disturbing statistics from the Vatican's statistical yearbook showing a 71 per cent decline in Canada's Catholic marriages from 1975–2008, more than double the decline of weddings in general. In the US, Catholic marriages decreased about 54 per cent from 1975–2010. Moreover, the Church is also challenged by a wedding reality far different from the classic nuptials of the 1950s and 1960s, with many couples coming to the altar having lived together and perhaps already with children.[5]

The Centre for Applied Research in the Apostolate (CARA) at Georgetown University in Washington, DC, has been tracking the phenomenon with the United States Conference of Catholic Bishops. World data collected from the Vatican's statistical yearbook and other sources indicate a 33 per cent decrease in Catholic marriages between 1970 and 2015. Similarly in Ireland, church marriages have declined, with

---

4   Mrozek and Mitchel, 'A healthy marriage culture builds a thriving society, studies show', *Prairie Messenger* (13 September 2017), p. 18.

5   Jean Ko Din, 'Church deals with declining number of weddings' (19 July 2017), p. 7.

Roman Catholic services falling from 16,854 in 2007 to 12,486 in 2016. There has been a comparable rate of decline in the Church of Ireland.

Conversely, civil ceremonies have risen from 4,762 to 6,156 in the same period. In 2011 a total of 269,800 ticked the 'no religion' box on the census form, but five years later 468,400 did so. That accounts for 10.1 per cent of the population. For the first time ever the percentage of Catholics in the Republic has dipped below 80 per cent: in 2016, 78 per cent said they were Roman Catholic, down from 84 per cent in 2011.

Other Christian denominations, however, showed increases in their number of followers: 126,414 people said they were members of the Church of Ireland, a 2 per cent increase on the 2011 figures, and 62,187 said they were Orthodox Christians, a 37 per cent increase (mostly due to the extension of the EU's freedom of movement rules to Romanian citizens in 2014). The Irish Jewish population has also risen by 30 per cent, to 2,557 members, and the number of people of the Islamic faith has seen an increase of 28.9 per cent in the five years between the 2011 and 2016 census.

We must keep this ongoing changing reality for many families and marriages in mind as we read the Pope's letter and this book, together with our own singular experiences of marriage and family in our own cultures, histories and ever-shifting political, economic and religious life in the world and the universal Church. We must remember to value all forms of partnerships and families and not fall into the trap of 'excessive idealization of marriage and family life'. It will be imperative to concentrate on the more pastoral concerns of the letter and the challenges that are offered, careful of actual circumstances of women, men and children living in diverse conditions of violence, poverty, sickness and upheaval worldwide. Families are much like star constellations. Where you stand and view them reveals different crucial aspects of their configurations and relationships.

Pope Francis prefaces his words in his Apostolic Letter saying:

It is my hope that, in reading this text, all will feel called to love and cherish family life, for 'families are not a problem; they are first and foremost an opportunity'.[6]

---

6   AL, 7, quoting 'Address at the Meeting of Families in Santiago de Cuba' (22 September 2015): *L'Osservatore Romano* (24 September 2015), p. 7.

It is my hope that this book will build on many of the ideas in Pope Francis' letter by reflecting on the scripture passages dealing with the origins of Jesus as the firstborn Child of God the Father, conceived by the Holy Spirit, and the stories we read most often in the season of Advent, Christmas and Epiphany, which we refer to as the stories and mysteries of the Annunciation, the Visitation, the Nativity, the Presentation, the Flight into Egypt and the Finding in the Temple.

For Christians and Catholics, once we are born into this world, whatever our family situation, we begin another step into the mystery of our lives in God with Baptism – all of us becoming the adopted beloved children of God when we are baptised into the Body of Christ. This is the first step into a new, powerful and life-creating kinship with God. We are initiated into the dynamic relationship that Jesus has with the Father in the power of the Spirit, called to be servants, disciples, friends and the beloved of God in this family that is reflective of the Trinity. We are reminded that the Spirit is the first gift given to those who believe. With this Spirit there is no limit to the imagination, the creativity, the life-giving expressions of what individuals and every human family can be and do for its immediate members and for all society, imitating Jesus' exhortation to 'be holy as our God is holy', echoing the Jewish call to holiness.

Again Pope Francis situates the entire letter to the Church regarding families in the context of hope and thanksgiving.

> I thank God that many families, which are far from considering themselves perfect, live in love, fulfil their calling and keep moving forward, even if they fall many times along the way. The Synod's reflections show us that there is no stereotype of the ideal family, but rather a challenging mosaic made up of many different realities, with all their joys, hopes and problems.[7]

As believers we are encouraged to become families who are servants of God, just and forgiving; families who are disciples that preach the Good News to the Poor (only as a last resort using words at the urging of St Francis of Assisi); families who become the friends of God, who do all that we have been commanded to do: loving one another as our God-

---

7   Ibid., 57.

Father has loved us in Jesus and remains with us in the Spirit of the Risen Jesus. We are called to always be more holy, more human, more like our home in God, in the Trinity.

In light of this, every father is a shadow of God the Father, every mother is overshadowed by the Spirit, and each child is a shadow of Jesus. Together every family reveals our God as Trinity, as family, as community, as Three in One, and One in Three. Every family in its diversity and uniqueness also has something to add to the revelation that is universal and necessary to our knowing more of our God. Alongside this amazing vocation of manifesting God in our families is the equally strong reality that every family and every individual in the family is severely limited, and we all fail and fall, and fail and fall, and yet we are still always holy and always seeking to become like Our Father, our Mothering Spirit and the Child, our brother Jesus. We dance through our lives, learn the steps, stumble, fall, pick ourselves up, or are helped up by others, dance with others, learn new steps, fall again and rise again.

Eva Burrows wrote, 'In family life, love is the oil that eases friction, the cement that binds closer together, and the music that brings harmony.' There are three roles that are crucial to family life: that of a father, that of a mother and a relationship of marriage – bonding together with one heart for the future – and that of the child. I remember my own mother saying forcefully to the six of us girls: 'You don't become a mother by giving birth. That's the day you begin to know how to mother someone.' And my father was adamant as well, 'The day your mother and I made love and you were conceived (before which you were a twinkle in the eye of God), I didn't become a father. That's the day I was invited to be your father. From that moment on, we were in this together for and with all of you.' From that moment on, each of us was 'one of his favourite daughters' or 'one of his favourite sons'. We started to become a family. That was more than seventy-five years ago and all of us are still becoming a family.

There is a story told in the Jewish community, though I have also seen a version of it from the Norbertine priest, Francis Dorf. It is about a monastery, which in some ways resembles a family, and how life rises and falls within its enclosure and its place in the world. It has many affinities to our conversation about how families grow.

Once upon a time there was an abbot of a monastery who was very good friends with the rabbi of a local synagogue. This was in Europe, and times were hard. Sometimes the rabbi would come and pour out his soul with the abbot and the abbot would encourage him; other times the abbot would visit his friend the rabbi and pour out his difficulties and be comforted by the rabbi.

The abbot found his community dwindling and the faith life of his monks shallow and lifeless. Life in the monastery was dying. He went to his friend and wept. His friend, the rabbi, comforted him and told him, 'There is something you need to know, my brother. We have long known in the Jewish community that the Messiah is one of you.'

'What?' exclaimed the abbot, 'The messiah is one of us? How can that be?'

But the rabbi insisted that it was so, and the abbot went back to his monastery wondering and praying, comforted and excited.

Once back in the monastery, walking down the halls and in the courtyard, he would pass by a monk and wonder if he was the one. Sitting in chapel, praying, he would hear a voice and look intently at a face and wonder if he was the one. And he began to treat all of his brothers with respect, with kindness and awe, with reverence. Soon it became quite noticeable.

One of the other brothers came to him and asked him what had happened to him. After some coaxing, he told him what the rabbi had said. Soon the other monk was looking at his brothers differently and wondering. The word spread through the monastery quickly; the Messiah is one of us. Soon the whole monastery was full of life, worship, kindness and grace. The prayer life was rich and passionate, devoted, and the psalms and liturgy and services were alive and vibrant. Soon the surrounding villagers were coming to services and listening and watching intently, and there were many who wished to join the community.

After their novitiate, when they took their vows, they were told the mystery, the truth that their life was based upon, the source of their strength and life together; the Messiah is one of us. The monastery grew and expanded into house after house, and all of the monks grew in wisdom, age and grace before the others and the eyes of God. And they say still, if you stumble across this place, where there is life and hope and kindness and graciousness, that the secret is the same; the Messiah is one of us.

The assortment of folk within the monastery relate in many ways as members of families: brothers, sisters, parents, visitors and relatives who are inter-generational and diverse. So to alter the way we look at one another can radically – at root – change how life is experienced and how all members of the family grow, mature and reflect back to others their singular expression of who God is, who dwells among us. As members of the Body of Christ, each of us is a mystery, a trace of the Trinity. God lives and dwells among us.

This process of becoming a family, a Christian family, has its fits and starts and is never-ending. It is a process of being born, struggling, dying, rising and being born again, following the Paschal Mystery that we celebrate as the heart of our religion and lives: the Incarnation, the life, dying, rising and indwelling of the Spirit of the Risen Lord as the first gift of the Father to all the families that are called to be holy, to be shadows of grace and icons of the Holy Trinity. At the very end of Pope Francis's letter, we are reminded:

The Lord's presence dwells in real and concrete families, with all their daily troubles and struggles, joys and hopes. Living in a family makes it hard for us to feign or lie; we cannot hide behind a mask. If that authenticity is inspired by love, then the Lord reigns there, with his joy and his peace. The spirituality of family love is made up of thousands of small but real gestures. In that variety of gifts and encounters which deepen communion, God has his dwelling place. This mutual concern 'brings together the human and the divine', for it is filled with the love of God. In the end, marital spirituality is a spirituality of the bond, in which divine love dwells.

A positive experience of family communion is a true path to daily sanctification and mystical growth, a means for a deeper union with God. The fraternal and communal demands of family life are an incentive to growth in openness of heart and thus to an ever fuller encounter with the Lord.[8]

---

8   AL, 315/316, quoting *Gaudium et Spes*, 49.

We carry our families with us as we mature and grow, begin our own families and watch one generation emerge into the next generation and on into history. Writer and theologian Frederick Buechner tellingly reminds us, 'You can kiss your family and friends goodbye and put miles between you, but at the same time you carry them with you in your heart, your mind, your stomach, because you do not just live in a world. A world lives in you.'

The closing words of Pope Francis's letter is a good place to begin – a jumping-off spot into our reflections and hopes for a deeper appreciation for Jesus' family of origin, the human family that came to an historical moment in the Holy Family of Jesus, Joseph and Mary. The words are visionary, but good for beginnings as a backdrop to all that we seek to know and experience as believers in the Trinity.

> As this Exhortation has often noted, no family drops down from heaven perfectly formed; families need constantly to grow and mature in the ability to love. This is a never-ending vocation born of full communion of the Trinity, the profound unity between Christ and his Church, the loving community which is the Holy Family of Nazareth, and the pure fraternity existing among the saints of heaven. Our contemplation of the fulfilment which we have yet to attain also allows us to see in proper perspective the historical journey which we make as families, and in this way to stop demanding of our interpersonal relationships a perfection, a purity of intentions and a consistency which we will only encounter in the Kingdom to come. It also keeps us from judging harshly those who live in situations of frailty. All of us are called to keep striving towards something greater than ourselves and our families, and every family must feel this constant impulse. Let us make this journey as families, let us keep walking together. What we have been promised is greater than we can imagine. May we never lose heart because of our limitations, or ever stop seeking that fullness of love and communion which God holds out before us.[9]

Let us end with the closing prayer of *Amoris Laetitia* as we look more closely at the members of the Holy Family we seek to know and imitate

---

9   Ibid., 325.

– each in our own singular ways, living out the presence of our God, and revealing faint traces of the One we were made to image, as we invite others to believe in their dignity as those who are created to give God delight.

Prayer To The Holy Family
Jesus, Mary and Joseph,
in you we contemplate
the splendour of true love;
to you we turn with trust.

Holy Family of Nazareth,
grant that our families too
may be places of communion and prayer,
authentic schools of the Gospel
and small domestic churches.

Holy Family of Nazareth,
may families never again experience
violence, rejection and division;
may all who have been hurt or scandalized
find ready comfort and healing.

Holy Family of Nazareth,
make us once more mindful
of the sacredness and inviolability of the family,
and its beauty in God's plan.

Jesus, Mary and Joseph,
Graciously hear our prayer.
Amen.

Chapter 2
The Annunciation to Mary

There is an ancient Native American legend called 'The Coming of the Light'. It is told in many traditions, but this version is closest to the Cherokee telling.

Once upon a time, long before any two-leggeds were in the world, the world was beautiful. But it was also pitch black. The animals could not see their way around. They were always falling into ruts and running into trees and knocking each other over and getting into fights. Eventually they started meeting in small groups and talking with one another.

'We can't go on living this way,' they said. 'This is not the way the Creator meant it to be. What we need is some light. What we need is some fire. We can't even see creation.'

Finally all the fish, birds and animals got together to talk over the situation (they could still all talk together in those days). They all agreed they needed light.

'Does anyone know where the light is?' they asked.

Raven swooped in and said: 'There is light way off in the east. Sometimes when I fly long and high, when I'm about exhausted, I can see the light just breaking in the east. Somebody has it – it's over there.'

The animals talked about it and thought of sending a delegation over to see about getting some of the light. But Fox broke in and said: 'If they have the light and have had it all this time and haven't shared it, they probably are selfish and won't share it with us. I think we'll have to steal it.'

The animals discussed this and decided that Fox was right.

But who was to go and steal it? They immediately decided that Buzzard should go. After all, Buzzard was strong and would last the journey. He wouldn't need to eat much along the way if he ate a lot before leaving. He could steal the light and bring it back.

Now Buzzard didn't look as he does today. In fact, Buzzard was beautiful. He had a great head of feathers, huge ones that shot straight up in the air, covering his whole head with rich, vibrant colours. He could fly high and fast. So they all gathered around and sent Buzzard off into the east.

Buzzard flew higher and longer than he'd ever flown before, and finally he saw the light in the east. He was tired, but he swooped down and grabbed a bit of fire and placed it on top of his head and headed off for the west and the waiting animals. As he flew, the wind fanned the flames. It grew really hot! By the time he swooped down to the animals waiting for him, the fire had gone out. And worse still, he'd lost all his beautiful head feathers. He was as bald and ugly as he is today. All the animals felt terrible, not only because they didn't get the light, but because Buzzard looked so awful. They realised how much he had lost on behalf of the community, and they tried to comfort him.

Then they discussed whom to send next. There was a murmur in the group, and Possum stepped forward, saying, 'I'm not as stupid as Buzzard. I'll steal the light, but I won't put it on my head. Besides, they'll be looking for someone now and watching the sky. I can go on the ground and blend in with the darkness and hide until the last minute.'

So off they sent him.

Now at that time Possum had a huge, bushy, beautiful tail. He headed east, found the light, grabbed a bit of it and placed it right in the middle of his great tail, and headed home as fast as he could move. He moved fast, smelling smoke and feeling really hot. By the time he got back to the animals, the fire had gone out again, and poor Possum had lost forever his great bushy tail. They all gathered around and comforted Possum, although Fox said, 'Oh, it's a shame you lost your beautiful tail, but I thought you said you weren't as stupid as Buzzard.' The animals were trying to be solicitous, but they were also getting frustrated. They really needed fire and light. Finally, a tiny little voice piped up and said, 'I'll go.'

Everyone looked around and said, 'Who is that?' It was Grandmother Spider.

She said again, 'I'll go. After all, they're going to be on guard now, and I am so small and inconspicuous that they won't even notice me. I'll go, rather slowly to the east, but I'll let out my spun thread and then find my way back in the dark. I'll bring back the fire. Who knows? Maybe I was created to bring light into the world.'

So they sent Grandmother Spider off to the east. She made her way very slowly, but as she went she gathered a little bit of wet clay and formed it into a small pot, which she placed upon her back. As she went into the east, it slowly dried and hardened. She continued along, leaving her trail behind her.

Although they were waiting and watching for someone to try to steal their light, they weren't expecting someone so small and quiet. Grandmother Spider stole in, took just a little bit of fire, and put it into her pot. Then she followed her own trail back home, rolling in her thread as she went.

The animals all knew she was coming, because as she drew near, the light spread, coming from the east until dawn arrived, the first day, on Grandmother Spider's back. Soon the light spilled out of the bowl and filled the whole sky. The animals took the little clay pot and announced, 'Grandmother, you have done what none of us could do. You have brought the light, the fire, and warmth into the world. We are grateful and we will honour you. From now on, spiders will remind us of the Creator's presence. And anyone who weaves and makes pots brings light into the world and continues creation's journey. We will remember.'

And so it is today. Among Native Americans, anyone who weaves and makes pots works with the Creator to hold the world together. And God is a great spider that weaves the web that holds us all together. They ask, 'Have you been caught in the web of the spider yet?'

This ancient story reveals belief in light, hope, the continuance of creation, the intercommunion of all that is made, and the meaning of certain creatures in the world. This creation story says much about how things got to be the way they are: how Buzzard got so ugly, why Possum has such a bare-looking tail, and how light came into the world. It also explains the connection between weavers and potters and the Creator. It speaks of a progression, a long history of attempts to obtain what is necessary for life, culminating in Grandmother Spider's small powers in doing what the more obvious powers of others could not.

What does this story have to do with Mary? For believers, all stories reveal the One Story, the coming of light into the world, who God is, who we are, how we are all connected, and why things are the way they are. All cultures and races and religions serve the one true God and reveal the Creator among us. Grandmother Spider says it clearly, simply and quietly, 'Maybe I was created to bring light into the world.' She does so with her quiet, small power, unnoticed by others, with creativity and imagination, using all she touches to bring the fullness of life to her people and setting in motion a trail of tradition for all weavers and potters and storytellers. This close-to-the-ground power of humility is necessary for all the earth's growth.

Always light comes from the east, the place of resurrection. In ancient baptismal rituals we are asked to turn and face the light that is coming upon us; we are baptised and given the light to take into the world, as Jesus brought light into the world, and as Mary, the first believer, brought light into the world. When the light comes, all is revealed.

In this story, light comes from a grandmother – old, wise and close to the earth. The grandmothers and grandfathers, the leaders of the community, sit on the earth and make decisions, knowing their choices will affect the next generations.

Perhaps Mary is Grandmother Spider. This remarkably different relationship reveals Mary as one who brings light and teaches us to grow up and do things for the larger community. She is grandmother of the earth and grandmother of the people of God. The Creator – and Mary – continue to weave the web that holds the world together. She expects us to do so as well.

According to tradition, Mary lived in the community at Ephesus until she was ninety-two years old. But grandmothers are more connected to a relationship than to a certain age. 'Grandmother' implies wisdom, understanding, patience, fortitude, enduring grace. In Native American traditions it is a high honour to be a person's grandmother, and a grandmother need not be a biological relative. Perhaps this relationship reveals as much about Mary as being mother, since this new family, this new community, is not based on biology but on wisdom, love, knowledge, affection, commitment, growth and support. Mary is not great because she is the physical mother of Jesus, but because she believes in Jesus.

In all our families, the women – grandmothers, mothers, sisters, aunts, nieces and girl children – are the ones that carry the shadow of the Spirit. They are the traces of light, of wisdom and love, truth and peace that circulate like air among all members of the family across generations.

The grandmother of the story is a spider! Spiders spin their webs out of the stuff of their own bodies. The web is there for catching unsuspecting creatures. Once in the web, the only way out is to get eaten by the spider or to tear a hole in the web. It seems the web of God works pretty much the same way.

Spiders travel with the wind and cover large distances. When their webs are destroyed, they spin again. Within a day's time the web is made anew. Research reports that spiders have the ability to alter their web patterns so that they become more and more strong and more and more capable of catching and holding both what they eat and what they are attached to. Webs are intricate, patterned and symmetrical. The material from which the web is spun is tough; relatively speaking, it is as strong as tensile steel. Native American women collect webs in late summer and early fall. They wad them together and use them to stop bleeding. The web of the Spider can stop the world from bleeding to death.

Many times webs can be seen only in certain kinds of light or with the dew or rain upon them. When Native Americans first saw globes of the world, they were struck by the lines encircling the earth. They assumed the navigators knew about the web of the Creator. They were soon informed that those lines were not the web that holds the world together, but the lines of latitude and longitude.

There are small signs in many reservation homes that say, 'Don't worry, God, I'm not a very good housekeeper'. Webs are allowed to stay because they are the presence of God within the dwelling place. When I first lived in New Mexico, I lived in an old adobe house and tried to honour the belief about spiders, but after being bitten a number of times and being a weak person, I tacked a sign to my bed, 'In the bed, you're dead!' Anywhere else they were allowed to take up residence.

Grandmother Spider's pot is made of earth, and it is earth that brings light to the world. We are made of earth, and with Mary we are to bring light into the world. Grandmother Spider and Mary have known the truth of Incarnation for a long, long time.

THE WOMAN OVERSHADOWED BY THE POWER OF THE MOST HIGH
Another version of the story of how light came into the world is contained in the first chapter of Luke's Gospel, which introduces us to Mary of Nazareth, Joseph – the man to whom she is engaged – and the angel Gabriel, the bearer of glad tidings. This reading is used for the Feast of the Annunciation, 24 March, and again nine months later, on the fourth Sunday of Advent. It is also the Gospel for the Feast of the Immaculate Conception, 8 December. It is the birth announcement of Jesus, the Son of God, also marking the end of the waiting, the end of old time. The Annunciation is celebrated in the northern hemisphere along with the coming of light into the darkness, near the winter solstice.

The angel Gabriel has been to earth often before, in the dreams of Daniel and others, and appearing to the priest Zechariah in the Temple in Jerusalem. As a result of that encounter, Zechariah is struck dumb for not believing. The description of the angel's words are strong and decisive, imperious, 'I am Gabriel, who stand before God, and I am the one sent to speak to you and bring you this good news! My words will come true in their time, although you would not believe. But now you will be silent and unable to speak until this has happened' (Lk 1:18-20).

His words too are soon shown to be truthful. Zechariah's ageing wife, Elizabeth, becomes pregnant with the promised son, the son who 'will be great in the eyes of the Lord … who will never drink strong wine but he will be filled with the Spirit even from his mother's womb. Through him many of the people of Israel will turn to the Lord their God. He himself will open the way to the Lord with the spirit and the power of the prophet Elijah; he will reconcile fathers and children, and lead the disobedient to wisdom and righteousness, in order to make ready for the Lord a people prepared' (Lk 1:15-17). The mysteries are set in motion, and the word spreads through the community that Zechariah has seen a vision.

Elizabeth 'for five months kept to herself, remaining at home, and thinking, "What is the Lord doing for me? This is his time for mercy and for taking away my public disgrace"' (Lk 1:23-25). Elizabeth has been barren, and as the wife of a priest this was a double disgrace. In Jewish society all theology and daily living revolved around the coming of the Messiah. To be barren was to exclude that possibility. Elizabeth undoubtedly spent a good deal of her life as an outcast, scorned and looked down upon. But now came the time of mercy.

> In the sixth month, the angel Gabriel was sent from God to a town of Galilee called Nazareth. He was sent to a young virgin who was engaged to a man named Joseph, of the family of David: and the virgin's name was Mary. (Lk 1:26-27)

'The virgin's name was Mary.' She is named. Traditionally the name Mary – Myriam – means 'sea of bitterness and sorrow', with 'sea' meaning the depths of water and psyche as well as the sea connected to the constant moon, tides and seasons. Historically Mary is a young woman, engaged to be married, from the backwater town of Nazareth in rural Galilee. But Mary is Jewish, and so she comes from a long tradition of strong, valiant women of faith and enduring hope, the undercurrent of Jewish life. And Mary is a virgin. This reference to the hope and promise of the prophets – that the Messiah would be born of a virgin in Israel (Is 7:14) – is more than a statement of biology. The stories of God, the stories of the believing Church, reveal not just history but faith, conversion and power for all believers.

The word 'virgin' has many meanings, a number of them more powerful and insightful than looking at Mary as 'a person (especially a woman) who has never had sexual intercourse'. Etymologically, the roots of the word are connected to the word 'virtue', from the word *vir*, meaning 'man'. The Romans derived the noun *virtus* to denote the sum of excellent human qualities, including physical strength, valorous conduct and moral rectitude. The French developed their word *vertu* or *virtu* from Latin, and it is first recorded in the tenth century. It came into English in the thirteenth century. In the fourteenth century 'virtue' came to be applied to any 'characteristic, quality, or trait known or felt to be excellent'. By the end of the sixteenth century, the sense 'chastity, purity' appeared, especially in reference to women.

Theologically, the term 'virgin' is connected to the long history of Israel, which is characterised as the woman, wife, beloved of Yahweh, who is more often unfaithful, wanton, worshipping other gods and sacrificing to other powers and forces. But Mary is a virgin. She is faithful, not like Israel with its long litany of infidelities. Mary is not just an individual Jew, but the woman of the Jewish people; she receives the promise for a virgin people, with a pure, single-minded heart.

Mary was ready for God. She was ready for all the people of Israel. She was ready for all those who waited! She goes before the people of God in waiting and hoping for the Messiah's arrival. She appears on the horizon of salvation as the Dawn of the Dayspring. From the very beginning her pilgrimage of faith has been 'a constant reference point for the Church, for individuals and communities, for peoples and nations and in a sense for all'.[1]

Mary is more than an historical person. She is also the Mother of the Church, the mothers of believers and disciples. In the Gospel of Luke, she best personifies the soul of each believer as he or she comes to experience the presence of God and assents to that presence by becoming a disciple of Jesus the Lord. It is Mary who reveals to us through her story the graciousness of God in creation and incarnation. She embodies more than any other the Christian response to God's goodness.

The process of becoming aware of God's redeeming love is often called *conscientizaçao* in liberation theologies. It is the process of becoming attentive to the present through reflection and praxis. Mary's experience of God and her relationship to Jesus, the Father, and the Spirit – and to all Christians – is the paradigm for all of us seeking to be disciples of Jesus, striving to embody in our flesh the Word of God. Whatever happens to Mary in these Gospel stories happens to every believer. Mary is the first disciple coming to believe in the word of the Lord.

Luke's community wrote its Gospel using Mary as image and symbol of belief. These first two chapters are the only place where Mary is named in Luke's Gospel. However, the entire Gospel has references to servants, the primary image of believers, and the way Mary describes herself: as handmaid, servant, or slave of the Lord. So, in reality, the entire Gospel is about Mary and about anyone who follows Jesus with her.

---

1 *Redemptoris Mater*, 6, John Paul II (25 March 1987).

The angel came to her and said, 'Rejoice, full of grace, the Lord is with you!' Mary listened and was troubled at these words, wondering what this greeting could mean.

But the angel said, 'Do not fear, Mary, for God has looked kindly on you. You shall conceive and bear a son and you shall call him Jesus. He will be great and shall rightly be called Son of the Most High. The Lord God will give him the kingdom of David, his ancestor: he will rule over the people of Jacob forever and his reign shall have no end.'

Then Mary said to the angel, 'How can this be if I am a virgin?' And the angel said to her, 'The Holy Spirit will come upon you and the power of the Most High will overshadow you; therefore, the holy child to be born shall be called Son of God. Even your relative Elizabeth is expecting a son in her old age, although she was unable to have a child, and she is now in her sixth month. With God nothing is impossible.' (Lk 1:28-37)

The first words that Mary hears are, 'Rejoice, full of grace, the Lord is with you.' Mary listened and was troubled at these words, wondering what this greeting could mean. This word 'rejoice' was the usual address for people in the city of Jerusalem, the community of the humble. She is not addressed by name but by the phrase 'full of grace' – favoured, chosen, beloved one. She is more than her name, even more than her person. She is all those called by God to bring forth the light.

Her response to this greeting is that she is troubled. There are a number of specific reasons why she was troubled. If she is what the angel claims, then who is she before God? Who is this God? What role does she play in God's creation? The angel responds immediately, 'Do not fear, Mary, for God has looked kindly on you and you shall conceive and bear a son and you shall call him Jesus.' Again, troubling words. She is engaged but unmarried. If what the angel says is true, she is in a dangerous position. Good, religious people will judge and condemn her.

And Joseph, what about Joseph? He is engaged to her and they are planning a life together. Now all that will be changed for them individually and as a couple. She has good reason to be disturbed. Once this Word of the Lord gets to her, gets inside her in even a seed form, her other life is over. This is true today for all of us. Whenever the Word penetrates our hearts and lives, our lives as we know them are over, as we begin anew.

She must choose without taking into consideration those she loves and with whom she lives.

The story continues to disturb her. The description is all about her child. It really has little or nothing to do with her, except that she is to call him Jesus. He will be the saviour, great and mighty and rightly called the Son of the Most High. The angel talks about who this child will be and what his names are, his relationship to the people and the rest of the world. Her choice is to say yea or nay, not just for her life and future, but for the life and future of the people. In this sense it is an impersonal announcement that leaves her out and points only to what will come forth from her if she agrees to God's favour and choice.

Mary's response reveals that she is aware of the enormity of this invitation and perhaps some of its demands politically, historically, religiously. Her response reveals acknowledgement of the child to be born, but questions how she, a woman in Galilee, engaged already to Joseph, of the house of David, can get from this moment to the future of her people. She is unwed and not sexually related as yet to Joseph, and so she asks, 'How?' The answer is a theological one, 'The Holy Spirit will come upon you and the power of the Most High will overshadow you: therefore the holy child to be born shall be called Son of God.'

To have the Holy Spirit come upon you and be overshadowed by the power of the Most High is no small thing in the history of the Jewish community. It is the announcement that the person is about to become a prophet, chosen by God to bring the Word of God to the people. Life, as she knows it, is over. The prophet has no life other than bringing forth the word of the Lord to the world.

In Mary's case, the word will not be in her mouth. She will give birth to the Word, a person of flesh and blood, made of her flesh and blood and the power and spirit of God, without recourse to a human father. The child is first of all God's, then the people's. She is being invited to speak on behalf of the people, to become the prophet that bears this word of hope to those long waiting in darkness and bondage.

There is the sense that she is troubled right up to the moment when she answers the angel. After all, Gabriel has a history with the Jewish people, found in the book of Daniel. Gabriel explains one of Daniel's visions to him, in obedience to the Word of God.

He [Gabriel] approached the place where I was. When he came, I was terrified and fell on my face. He said to me, 'Son of man, understand: this vision refers to the end-time.' As he spoke, I lost consciousness and fell face down on the ground. He touched me and raised me to my feet. Then he said, 'See, I will reveal to you what is going to happen when the wrath comes to an end, for the end is set.' (Dn 8:17-19)

The vision is revealed in detail, and Daniel is told to keep the vision secret. In the next chapter Gabriel is clear about what will happen and what must be done. Daniel is praying. It is the hour of the evening sacrifice, and Daniel is confessing his sins and those of the people, begging Yahweh on behalf of his Holy Mountain and people. Gabriel comes to Daniel and says:

Daniel, I have come now to make you understand. As you were praying, a word was uttered and I have come to teach it to you because God loves you. Pay attention to this word and understand the vision: seventy weeks are set for your people and your holy city, to put an end to transgression, to wipe out the offence, and to bring everlasting justice, so that the visions and the prophecies will be fulfilled and the Holy of Holies be anointed. (Dn 9:22-24)

Thus Gabriel is associated with judgement and the coming of justice, the time of salvation for the world and the end of other time. Mary, by the power of the Spirit, is awakened to the promises and power of the prophets coming to fulfilment in her time. She is aware that she is bound to the nation of Israel, the holy ones of God, who wait on his word to come in fullness. This is not just about her individual choice. This is about history being interrupted and God intervening, altering the present and recreating the world forever. Something radical is about to happen. The reign of God is coming upon the world, and this reign will have no end. This is salvation and judgement and the coming of justice in a person; it will be so clear that all the world will see the light in the Jewish community. This child is connected first to the people and through the people to her. She is one of the holy ones of God. Like Daniel, she will hide the vision, the secret, until its time, until birth. This child is the Son of Man described in the book of Daniel. He is Emmanuel, God with us. And he is more than anyone was expecting.

Mary is given another piece of information 'Even your relative Elizabeth is expecting a son in her old age, although she was unable to have a child, and she is now in her sixth month. With God nothing is impossible' (Lk 1:36-37). Are these words of comfort, explanation, information, or the intimation that the mystery is set in motion? Or does Mary need a place to go that is safe, where the secret will be safe from prying and misunderstanding eyes? Is Elizabeth's house her sanctuary, a place to catch her breath as well as a place to learn what it means to be pregnant from an older woman in an awkward position too? After all, Elizabeth is an old pregnant woman – highly unlikely, a bit bizarre. And Mary, a virgin, will be pregnant by the Spirit of God – harder still to believe. The impossible is starting to happen, and there is much more to come. This is only the beginning. From here on out all of history, all of reality, even all of religion changes. God is moving in closer than ever before, into our bodies and hearts and souls. Once inside, in the body and heart of Mary, God will stay forever in the children born of water and the spirit, after being born of flesh and blood.

The story concludes as Mary responds 'I am the servant of the Lord, let it be done to me as you have said.' And the angel left her.

It is done, irreversible, time altered, incarnation. God is made flesh and dwells among us. God is human and hiding in the world in a woman of Nazareth, a town in the middle of nowhere, among a people oppressed and burdened and of little or no worth, chosen and favoured to bring light into the world and shatter the darkness. Mary surrenders, obeys – she has listened, heard and taken the words to heart, so single-mindedly that the Word becomes flesh in her. In a moment it is done. She is mother, maid-servant, prophet, bearer of hope to her people, a light to the nations – and in danger.

In the Gospel of Luke, the annunciation is the only time Mary sees or hears the angel or has the vision. From now on she lives with the Word, surrendering in obedience to an ever-growing and maturing understanding of the Word in her life and in the world. The seed is planted, and it will bear fruit in her child and in her life as disciple and believer.

Immediately she sets out for Jerusalem, toward sanctuary, toward Elizabeth. She believes, and she sets off to find a way to make the vision come true. She is the image of the one who incarnates, makes flesh and blood the reality of God in the world. She is *Theotokos*, the God-bearer. She is the first of Jesus' disciples, those chosen to bring light and hope into a world in desperate need of salvation.

Mary gives her word and keeps it. Her life is no longer defined by being a virgin engaged to Joseph. She is a servant of the living God, a prophet of the Most High, the bearer of the seed of justice and judgement and the hope of the nations. Her new life, her new relationship to God, has begun. She lives now on the Word and obeys, doing for God and her people what they have believed in and hoped for ages.

'Let it be done to me as you have said.' This is Mary's acknowledgement of belief, her Baptism, her confession of faith, her proclamation of hope in God. They are the words of the Christian community in her mouth: a post-resurrection statement of Christ, the Lord, the Son of God. She is the first person to hear the Gospel and take it to heart. She believes in what God will do, in her child to come. She believes it changes everything, including first of all who she is and what she is to be. She is the highly favoured daughter of God, full of grace.

Each of us shares that moment of belief with Mary at our Baptism, when we too become the children of God, full of grace and freedom, by the power of the Spirit that overshadows us and comes to dwell with us. This woman, Mary, of Luke's Gospel presents us with the presence of the Spirit in our flesh throughout our lives. She reveals to us that every woman in our families embodies the light of the living Spirit of God.

A few years ago, travelling in Wales, I did a parish mission in a dark, poor small town, made nearly all of slate mined in the hills above the area. At night in the home of my host, we would sit by the fire, drinking a bit of whiskey and watching the sky darkening and the shadows coming on. It was fascinating. The house was high in the hills above the town. First there would be one light. Then the minutes would pass and another light, then another. A trail of light wound its way below us, around and in and out. I watched, wondering what it was and how it was created. My host smiled and said, 'Ah, you've noticed. We are still poor here. That is the lamplighter, walking through town, lighting the gas lamps.' Then he said, 'There is a saying by John Ruskin that I always recall when

I catch sight of the lamps being lit down below in the town "You always know you have been in the presence of a Christian by the trail of light they leave behind".' I was stunned.

The light still makes its way in the world, quietly, anonymously, by the small and the powerless servants of God, and the earth still rejoices at its arrival as it penetrates the darkness of our souls, our minds and our lives. Grandmother Spider's comment applies to all of us; perhaps we were created to bring light into the world.

Chapter 3
The Visitation: The Shadow Lengthens

THE GREETING

The story of Mary's visit to Elizabeth begins abruptly, 'Mary then set out for a town in the hills of Judah.' This is the first of three journeys that Mary will make to Jerusalem, recounted in the first two chapters of Luke. In a sense, these chapters mirror the journeys of soul and spirit that each believer makes in imitation of Jesus.

In this first trip Mary is pregnant and alone, travelling the ninety miles to the outskirts of Jerusalem. She will stay for three months, until the birth of John, and then return to Nazareth. Then she will go again to the outlying districts of Jerusalem, with Joseph, when she is much farther along in her pregnancy, so that her child is born in Bethlehem. Third, she and Joseph will take Jesus to the Temple in Jerusalem for Jesus' appearance before the priests and elders when he is around twelve, at his bar mitzvah, his coming of age as a Jewish adult.

For the first journey, Mary leaves immediately after the annunciation. The angel has given her one small piece of practical information: her relative Elizabeth is already six months along in her pregnancy, even though she was barren all these past years and is old, past the years of bearing a child. Elizabeth's house is ninety miles away, safe from prying eyes; besides, there is already talk of Elizabeth and Zechariah and what this child of theirs will be. So she goes. She acts on faith. She goes to serve her relative in need. She is moved by compassion and her own need, and she immediately responds. She will be a help to Elizabeth, but Elizabeth will be a help to her as well. Elizabeth will understand more than others that they are part of a larger piece of history and promise. They will be *con-spirators*, people who 'breathe together' to bring something hidden into the world. So a young virgin who is pregnant and unmarried and an old, barren woman who is now pregnant will encounter one another and live together for a while as friends. This is the beginning of the story, strange enough to give us due warning that from here on out the story will grow more mysterious, a story of faith and belief, enacted in our own lives as much as in the lives of Mary and Elizabeth.

The first thing we note from the story of Incarnation is that when the good news breaks into history, our life and relationships are deeply disturbed. Mary is great because she gives birth to and brings the Word to the world. But this is the vocation of every believer. The power of the Most High overshadows and the Spirit comes upon each of us, sending us out into the world and history to bring the Word to life and flesh in us.

Like Mary, we begin by asking how. This is the Catechumenate, the time of asking questions and receiving theological answers to wrap our practical life around. The questioning is about her relationship to the Trinity, Father, the Most High, the Shadow of the Spirit, and her child, Jesus. Her response is theological, 'I am the servant of the Lord.' In Luke's Gospel, Jesus is the Suffering Servant of the Lord, and all references in the Gospel to the servants tell us about Mary and about ourselves. 'So you also. When you have done all that you have been told to do, you must say, "We are not more than servants; we have only done our duty"' (Lk 17:10). It is an attitude of worship, of service, of obedience, of belonging to entirely; our life is not our own. It is based on the word of the one who owns us.

Mary is the servant, prophet, virgin mother bearing the Word into the world, a very hostile world. To bear this child is to bear the cross and to bear her share of bringing the Gospel into history. She is a disciple of Jesus, her child, the Son of the Most High. What God called Mary to be, we are called to be as well. We are called back again and again, ritually, sacramentally and in the proclamation of the Word in our midst. The first part of the story is familiar.

> Mary then set out for a town in the hills of Judah. She entered the house of Zechariah and greeted Elizabeth. When Elizabeth heard Mary's greeting, the baby leapt in her womb. Elizabeth was filled with the Holy Spirit, and giving a loud cry, said, 'You are most blessed among women and blessed is the fruit of your womb! How is it that the mother of my Lord comes to me? The moment your greeting sounded in my ears, the baby within me suddenly leapt for joy. Blessed are you who believed that the Lord's Word would come true!' (Lk 1:39-45)

Elizabeth recognises her Lord and the mother of her Lord. She is in relationship to the Spirit in that moment of insight and knowledge. She blesses Mary because of the Lord God, and because she has believed that the Lord's word would come true. Elizabeth's relationship to Mary is based on belief and hope, on their shared faith and on waiting. Belief is expressed in action, in response to hearing the word. Elizabeth senses the truth about Mary, who brings with her the presence of God, and they are one in the Spirit.

Even as Mary greets Elizabeth, the sound of her voice and the force of her presence evokes joy, leaping and dancing. Jesus, in John's Gospel, describes his own Spirit as 'rivers of living water leaping up and flowing like a fountain from within him' (Jn 7:39). This Spirit of Jesus in Mary causes John, the child in Elizabeth's womb, to take notice and leap and kick. This is the one for whom he and all the prophets have been waiting. Two women's belief in the word has set in motion the recreation of the world, the revolution of power and redemption.

In the Eastern Church this feast of the Visitation is called the Embrace or the Kiss, and the icons depict Mary and Elizabeth warmly, fondly embracing each other. Their faces and figures are radiant, the presence seeping out of their bodies into the air itself, uncontainable in their flesh. The Spirit in the early Church was called 'the Kiss of the Mouth of God' and these two believers kiss ecstatically and embrace one another. The mystery envelops them completely.

Mary goes to Elizabeth and is recognised as she truly is, as God sees her and relates to her. Elizabeth is friend to Mary, accepting her, recognising her, affirming her, and blessing her. Mary can only sing!

The process of believing is shared and extensive. All of us are blessed likewise in not being alone in our belief, in having a friend or friends who give us the freedom to sing and proclaim the glory of God in us, others in whose presence we know we are loved and honoured. Elizabeth is the first to honour Mary; all of us follow in her wake. We sing the praises of Mary as we sing the praises of God and rejoice that we are a part of that wonder, that mystery of salvation unfolding. Mary's belief is acknowledged and strengthened by another's faith. We too grow in our awareness of who we are and who God is and what it means to obey. It is others who call us forth and give to us the occasion to pray aloud and worship God with them. Mary's visit, her going to serve another in need and to learn what she is soon to experience, is returned by hospitality and gracious praise and welcome. The journey is completed with prayer and prophecy.

Mary sings, but she does not sing only for herself. She sings for her people. She preaches in song and joy. She prophetically announces what is to come, what will take place in the future, and what is already beginning in her flesh and blood. She speaks of her child and the three turnings, the three revolutions that he will set in motion in the world: the turning of the heart, the turning of politics and power, and the turning of hunger and economics.

In Elizabeth's presence Mary can sing, borrowing from the ancient traditions of Israel, the battle song of Hannah (from Samuel) and about what God does in history, using simple folk who believe and hope. She is careful to begin:

> My soul proclaims the greatness of the Lord, my spirit exults in God my saviour! He has looked upon his servant in her lowliness and people forever will call me blessed. The Mighty One has done great things for me, Holy is his Name! From age to age his mercy extends to those who live in his presence.

She is great because God has taken notice of her. God thinks of her! She is not great because of anything she does or will do, but because God includes her in the marvellous work of salvation and wonders. And so she proclaims aloud the great works of God and what has been done for her, in her, and what God will do in her child for the rest of the world. She is prophet, and she comes right to the point: God has acted with power and done wonders, scattering the proud with their plans.

The first turning, the first revolution will be that of consciousness, of awareness, of personal conversion. All of us, in the conceits of our hearts, our depths, where we lay our plans and set up our agendas and security, will be touched and turned upside down. Our conversion is first priority with God.

The second turning builds on the first, 'He has put down the mighty from their thrones and lifted up those who are downtrodden.' Mary proclaims the change that is to take place in the human condition. As Martin Luther King, Jr., said:

> Despite the fact that all too often people see in the Church a power opposed to any change, in fact, the Church preserves a powerful ideal which urges people towards the summits and opens their eyes as to their own destiny. From the hot spots of Africa to the black areas of Alabama, I have seen men and women rising and shaking off their chains. They had just discovered they were God's children, and that, as God's children, it was impossible to enslave them.

The poor and lowly are capable of toppling oppressive powers, no matter how great, provided they do not use the weapons of the rich and the violent.

The song of Mary also expresses the deepest feeling of the Christian soul. There is a time for us to seek truth, to discover what our major duties are, and to become truly and essentially human. There is a time for asking from and serving God. We come to understand that divine love seeks out that which is poorer and weaker in order to fill it and make it great.

This second turning is that of political understanding of power. Here God is proclaimed loudly to be on the side of the poor, the meek ones of the earth, the oppressed, the silent, the ones with no power. They will be lifted up and they will be blessed, for they shall inherit the earth!

The third turning is this, 'He has filled the hungry with good things but he has sent the rich away empty.' Those who hunger and thirst for justice will have their fill. This third turning is that of economics, of resources, of food, of distribution of land and wealth. It echoes the kingdom coming, the work of the long-awaited one, the one who saves. In Mary's mouth are the words that Jesus will quote from Isaiah when he first proclaims his mission in the synagogue in Nazareth:

> The Spirit of the Lord is upon me. He has anointed me to bring good news to the poor, to proclaim liberty to the captives and new sight to the blind; to free the oppressed and announce the Lord's year of mercy. (Lk 4:18-21)

Mary sings alone on a hill with only an old woman and unborn children to hear what her child will proclaim boldly three decades later in the local synagogue. He learned the song well and sang it surely. These are the first public words of Jesus in Luke. The preaching of Jesus and the words of Mary's Magnificat are stanzas from the same song of freedom and liberation.

Mary sings that God will do great things for the earth, for already this God has done great things for her. She begins, as all people do, with the right to being, a right to become fully human in this world, with the right to sing. She has a right to joy and greatness and a life without fear and oppression, a right to bear children who will grow up in wisdom and age and grace before the world. Mary is great because the Word has captured her being, her soul, and claims her first for God and then for the earth and the earth's children. We too are great in this same way, following as disciples.

In the Hebrew tradition God would remember an evil done down to the third and fourth generation, but good was remembered to the thousandth generation. Mary reminds all generations to come that God 'is remembered for his mercy, even as he promised.' All generations will know this powerful mercy. If we become servants who remember that we are only great because of what God does in us, as God comes through us into the world, then we will be great and God will lift up his lowly ones to seat them in glory. This has all the intimations of the prophet Isaiah's words about the Suffering Servant being lifted up and drawing all things to himself (on the cross) and then the Father lifting him in glory and seating him at the right hand of God.

Mary sees herself not so much as Jesus' mother, but as one of his people. She aligns herself with those faithful people, a remnant of hopeful ones, obedient and waiting for the glory of God to be made manifest. Today Mary still aligns herself with the lowly ones of earth, those who struggle for justice and peace, those who struggle against governments and inequality, against violence, greed, selfishness, pride and power. She sides with the lowly, the meek, the hungry, the non-violent, the single-hearted, the merciful, the peacemakers, the poor and those thirsting for justice and friendship with God. She is the woman of the Beatitudes, the woman of the Magnificat, the singing woman delighting in what God is doing and thoroughly delighted that she has a part in this work and dance.

The kingdom is here. It exists on a hill outside Jerusalem, in an old woman pregnant with a child who will lose his head at a dinner party while others dance to the tune of the world's powers, and in a young, unmarried, pregnant woman, carrying a child who will die horribly, only to rise and confound the world forever. Four prophets standing on a hillside, hiding the power of God in their flesh, in the old, the unborn, the unmarried mothers and the poor. This power lurks in poor places, on the edge of dominant cultures and power, waiting for its time of fulfilment. There are only a few who know that it grows stronger and stronger until the time is ripe and it is here. But it is in our midst even now, and one day all the world will have to recognise it and accept this power and be judged by its standards and priorities.

Mary is a believer. Her life is based on trust and the knowledge that is available from the tradition of the people and the power of the Spirit. She knows the prophets, the psalms, the promises and the depth of her people's history and pain. She is drawn into the one God, the Trinity, in the same way we are drawn in, through the Word and the experience of our obedience to the Word and the community. She learns as she goes along, as a member of a believing community. She sings, and the words that come from her mouth come true in the world. She sings God into existence in some mysterious and marvellous way.

There is a tribe in east Africa in which the art of true intimacy is fostered even before birth. In this tribe, the birth date of a child is not counted from the day of its physical birth or the day of conception, as in other village cultures. For this tribe the birth date comes the first time the child is a thought in its mother's mind. Aware of her intention to conceive a child with a particular father, the mother goes off to sit alone under a tree. There she sits and listens until she can hear the song of the child that she hopes to conceive. Once she has heard it, she returns to her village and teaches it to the father, so that they can sing it together as they make love, inviting the child to join them. After the child is conceived, she sings it to the baby in her womb. Then she teaches it to the old women and the midwives of the village, so that throughout the labour and at the miraculous moment of birth itself, the child is greeted with its

song. After the birth, all the villagers learn the song and sing it to
the child when it falls or hurts itself. The song becomes a part of
the marriage ceremony when the child is grown. And, at the end
of life, his or her loved ones will gather around the deathbed and
sing this song for the last time.[1]

Mary sings her child's song throughout her life. It is the song she hummed
as she rocked the child in the cave of Bethlehem. She sang it as she
walked home the night he was murdered and buried. Perhaps she sang
it every evening and morning of her life until she went home at last to
the fullness of the kingdom and the fulfilment of the words she had lived
so untiringly and faithfully.

Do our voices, our greetings to one another in our meetings, stir the
Spirit to life and cause us together to cry out in joy and praise of God? Is
our belief validated by the acknowledgement and shared faith of others
in the community? Do we respond to this confirmation of our belief by
proclaiming the good news aloud to all who would be open to hearing it?
Mary is seen as the Mother of the Church because her child is the leader
and the protector of the least, the poorest among us. Oscar Romero, the
Archbishop of San Salvador, would remind his people over and over again
in his sermons: 'A Church that does not join the poor in order to speak
out from the side of the poor against the injustices committed against
them is not the true Church of Jesus Christ.' For many in the Church of
Central and Latin America, in fact in many places around the world, Oscar
Romero is a symbol of what it means to be overshadowed by the Spirit.
He is seen and honoured as a Mother of the Church of the poor. In the
realm and the power of the Spirit men are made mothers bringing others
to birth. And we will see that it is the same with Joseph as father – women
are made fathers by the grace and favour of the Spirit.

Later in Luke's Gospel, just before Jesus goes into Jerusalem to die,
he will mourn and lament over the whole city. We do not often connect
the magnificat song of Mary with the lamentation of Jesus but they are
intimately bound together.

---

1   Adapted from Jack Kornfield, *A Path With Heart* (New York: Bantam, 1993).

As he drew near, he saw the city and wept over it, saying, 'If this day you only knew what makes for peace – but now it is hidden from your eyes. For the days are coming upon you when your enemies will raise a palisade against you; they will encircle you and hem you in on all sides. They will smash you to the ground and your children within you, and they will not leave one stone upon another within you because you did not recognise the time of your visitation.' (Lk 19:41-45)

The same word, 'visitation', is used – Jesus will come to meet his people and they will miss his coming. The account of Jesus' coming into the city is even more material and profound in Matthew. He cries out:

Jerusalem, Jerusalem, you who kill the prophets and stone those sent to you, how many times I yearned to gather your children together, as a hen gathers her young under her wings, but you were unwilling! Behold, your house will be abandoned, desolate. I tell you, you will not see me again until you say, 'Blessed is he who comes in the name of the Lord.' (Mt 23:37-39)

Another visitation, and this one carries a beatitude, a blessing as well – Mary came bearing Jesus in her womb. John will go before the face of the Lord to prepare his way. Jesus will go before all the people, knowing they will cry out blessings upon him, but they will not recognise his visitation or take his word and his presence into their hearts.

Whenever I read this portions of the Word I am reminded of a plant called 'the hen and chicks' or 'hen-and-biddies'. It is a small group of succulent plants that flower only once, native to southern Europe and northern Africa. They grow very close to the ground, nesting around one another so they appear to be one flower in the shape of a rosette or a rose window. All their offsets are 'chicks', with the hen being the main or mother plant, but they soon bud, then sprout their own roots, move in to stay near the mother plant but propagating quickly. There are innumerable varieties, and they are 'tough' plants, hugging the ground, growing best around rocks, even in rocky soil. When I looked them up, the last thing that was mentioned was that they grow best in light shade! An apt image of Jesus in Mary, John in Elizabeth and all of us giving birth to God. As

Bede the Venerable said many centuries ago: 'A soul that has believed has both conceived and bears the Word of God and declares God's works. Let the spirit of Mary be in each of you, so that it rejoices in God.'

Mary stays with Elizabeth about three months and then returns home. She stays long enough to learn what she needs to know in her own life, about birthing, about coming to the fullness of time herself. Mary is one of the midwives to Elizabeth in birthing John. She stays for the feasting and the naming and the joyous return of Zechariah's voice and his song to the goodness of God, when he is full of the Spirit. All the echoes are there: mercy, salvation from enemies, a victorious saviour being raised up, promises coming true, being called to be servants. Then Mary returns to Nazareth, returning to the outskirts of Jerusalem only when it is time for her child to be born.

There are practical questions we need to ask. If Mary stayed with Elizabeth for three months at the beginning of her pregnancy, why does she give birth in a cave outside the city, in Bethlehem, and live on the outskirts of the city until the family flees in terror from Herod? Why didn't she stay with Elizabeth and Zechariah and share her joy with them? And if all boys under the age of two were slaughtered, how does John survive? We don't know the answers. But we do know these are stories of faith, of conversion and of remembrance much more than of history or mere fact. Each piece is an invitation to deeper belief and challenging response to life.

There is a tradition today among Palestinian Christian and Muslim women. They bring their children under the age of three to Ein Karim, the Shrine of the Visitation, six miles north of the city of Jerusalem. The women bring their children to pray and ask blessings for them. However, they do not go into the church itself. Instead, they climb the hills behind the church where there are rocks and caves. They sit in the caves, hidden, in the memory of Elizabeth, who, they say, during the slaughter of the children climbed into the hills, lived in the caves and cried out to God to save her child. Now they, twenty-first-century Palestinian Christian and Muslim women, hide in the caves and pray to God that their children will be spared from the slaughter taking place today.

Scripture stories are not primarily history. They are theology, stories of God that make it easier for us to believe and come to a deeper awareness of how God works in history. They reveal our role in revealing the wonders of God to the earth. They encourage us to take risks. Mary is a prophet, and calls us to be prophets. Mary sings, and we are called to sing, borrowing her words and making them ours. We must learn to stand side by side with Mary and sing the Magnificat with her, proclaiming aloud what God has done for us and what God will do with us in the world. Mary was overshadowed by the Spirit. Mary is always saying: 'Don't stop with me. Keep going into God. I am who I am because God is who God is.' That truth and mystery are shared with us in grace. We are invited into the same kind of intimacy with God that Mary knew, in the same way – through hearing and believing the word of the Lord and putting it into practice in our lives now. We too are overshadowed by the Spirit. God will gladly give us anything we need to help us. We are cared for with great tenderness and sent to care for others who have not experienced this word of hope and justice yet. Like Mary, we will be remembered for the mark we leave behind, for the words we sing and believe in and make come true in our lives. We will be remembered for all the 'chicks' we set on their way.

Now there are two women, shadows of the Spirit carrying their children within them, on the edge of shifting and changing all the history of the world. Two women prophets. Prophets have always hinted that certain people know where God hangs out. They speak of specific groups of people mentioned in the holiness code of the Jewish Torah: the widows, the orphans, the old, the illegal aliens in our midst, the migrants, the prisoners, the oppressed, those who are the misfits of traditional society, and those bereft and alone. We lump them all together and call them 'the poor'. God hears their cry and bends down very close to them. God bends close to Mary and Joseph, Elizabeth and Zechariah (later Simeon and Anna and the shepherds), all who are the very poor. If God is going to come among us as we celebrate in every Advent, Christmas and Epiphany season in our families, in our parishes and in the world, it usually won't be announced first to the great and the mighty. God will go – as always – to the people who already know God is in the world – to ordinary folk, to the good people, to families and to those actually waiting for him.

The Incarnation and Annunciation stories say that God is hidden in us. Mary believes that part of the story, as unbelievable as it is. She believes too that Elizabeth, an old woman, is now pregnant. She believes that she, a virgin, has conceived a child. Her child is going to be human and the child of God too. That's still harder for us to believe. This child is going to be killed when he grows up for preaching the good news to the poor ones of the earth, but he is going to be raised from the dead. That's even harder to believe. We are all invited into the relationship that her son will have with his Father-God, and we too live that resurrection life already, right now, because of our Baptism. That's hard to believe, but that's the way the story goes.

When asked, Mary said yes. We can almost imagine Mary looking at the angel Gabriel and saying: 'Tell God I say yes.' But we also are invited and asked – and every one of us says yes in our Baptism. We all tell God we'll obey. We say yes. Often times we think, what does my one small life mean? I'm just one of billions and billions of people. There is a story told among peacemakers, but among all who believe the most outrageous things about being human, about being mothers, fathers, even children who believe that God is one of us and what each of our small lives can mean.

Once upon a time there were two birds sitting on a branch of a tree. One was a dove and one was a titmouse (a small grey bird, sort of like a sparrow). They were sitting and talking about all the things that were going on in the world. They had heard stories from all over as they migrated and visited with other birds, and they were exchanging the news. Then, as was their habit, they began to discuss philosophy and theology and politics. But after a while they became bored with that.

Then it began to snow. It was the kind of snow that brought fat, fluffy flakes. The dove looked at the titmouse and asked: 'Do you know how much a snowflake weighs?'

The titmouse thought about it awhile and said, 'No, I never thought about it.'

'Well,' said the dove, 'I think it weighs nothing more than nothing. I mean, look at the snow floating down, these fat, soft, fluffy flakes.'

The titmouse thought about it some more and said, 'If you think a snowflake weighs nothing more than nothing, I have a little story to tell you. Once when I was sitting on a branch, just like this one, I didn't have anything to do. It started to snow, so I began counting snowflakes, fat and fluffy ones just like these ones. I counted a lot, a couple of hundred, a couple of thousand. I got up to one million, eight hundred and forty-six thousand, six hundred and twenty-two snowflakes, and then one snowflake – which you say weighs nothing more than nothing – floated down, landed on my branch, and cracked it straight through. The branch went falling to the ground, and I had to fly off.'

With that the titmouse flew off and left the dove sitting alone on the branch.

The dove, who has always been associated with peace, sat there trying to figure out the story. Suddenly it dawned on her. Of course. One snowflake, one person, when added to all the others, may be the one that makes all the difference in the world.

What if we, each of us, tell God that we too say yes? If we do, perhaps the story will come true in ways none of us ever thought about, and the world will know that nothing is impossible with God – and that God needs us to make all the stories come true, each of us, in our families in our world today. The Spirit of God comes to each of us, to overshadow us, to put up the tent over us and our families, teaching us to sing together the glories of our God and all the amazing things our God is going to do for us and with us. God is always remembering us.

Chapter 4
The Annunciation to Joseph the Just

THE SHADOW OF THE FATHER

Matthew's stories of the Annunciation and the Incarnation are in sharp contrast to Luke's beginning. Matthew's account begins with Joseph and dreams, rather than Mary and angels. It is the earlier account of the origins of the birth of Jesus, told to a primarily Jewish community in the process and throes of becoming more diverse, including gentiles. Matthew's community was becoming a more universal Church, seeking to have the original community evolve into Christians no longer waiting for the Messiah and dependent solely on the Law and the Prophets in the Torah, but now following Jesus and living as children of God and brothers and sisters of Jesus who, with him, in the power of the Spirit, call God our Father.

This story is about the history that surrounds the birth of Jesus, the Messiah, but it is also the history that is the backdrop for the birth of any child. And it becomes the story of Joseph in the long tradition of Judaism. It too is a story about hope, about the discovery of a promise coming true, about the fulfilment of the scriptures. It begins with the introduction of Joseph the just, appearing immediately after the genealogy in Chapter 1 of Matthew's Gospel. We begin there because it is also about this man Joseph, who has the soul of a child, believes in God's dreams and surrenders his entire life and strength to making sure that the dream comes true in his life and family.

We begin with a traditional Jewish story about a man called Joseph.

Once upon a time, during the days when God appointed Judges to rule over Israel, the Ark of the Covenant was lost for a short time. Without this touchstone of the presence of God with his people, the tribes were growing lax in their worship. This was where God dwelled with them, where they gathered together as one people. The leaders and priests decided they had to have a new ark until the original one was found. So, the word went forth to all the people to make a place where God would stay with them. All the artists, craftsmen and carpenters were invited to build one, which they would then bring together. It would be God Himself who would chose the one He would enter.

After a time, the day appointed came and everyone brought their arks to the meeting place. There were so many! Crafted of wood, stone, bronze, silver, gold and ornamented with every kind of jewel, inlaid tiles, carved with intricate designs, edged with ivory, ebony, lined with cedar and every kind of silk and cloth. How would they choose from such an array? The high priest and his servants went around and stood before each ark and cast their die to determine the Lord's choice. Again and again, an ark was not accepted. Then they approached a simple wooden chest with no carving or decoration. It was a simply made box. But when the die was cast it was chosen! Everyone was upset, including the priests. Who had made this ark? A poor man, a labourer who fashioned pieces of leftover or found wood stepped forward. His name was Joseph and he acknowledged that it was his work and that he had made it with deep devotion and intense hope that God would dwell within it.

There were arguments and discussions among the priests and people. The leaders were adamant that God deserved the best, not this piece that anyone could have made. They shouted and claimed that if this is where our God dwells among us, what will the other nations and religions think? They'll say our God is ordinary, without majesty, without power, without strength – nothing like our God. So, they went and threw the die again, in procession, before all the other arks. And once again it only fell to Joseph's: and then a third time. Only Joseph's found favour. As they continued to argue, a prophet raised his voice. God has chosen. Who are we to refuse the will of our God? God has chosen Joseph's ark because of his labour, his humble obedience and devotion and his faith. When we come before him we will not be distracted by outward appearances, but we will, instead, bow before Him and think only of Him, as Joseph does, and so God settled on Joseph's labour of love.

The story reveals many of the characteristics of Joseph, the father of Jesus, who is described as an upright or just man. This Joseph carries echoes of another Joseph, in the book of Genesis. In the genealogy we read: 'and Jacob the father of Joseph the husband of Mary, of whom Jesus was born, who is called the Messiah' (Mt 1:17b). But early on in this family tree we read: 'Abraham was the father of Isaac, and Isaac the father of Jacob, and Jacob the father of Judah and his brothers' (Mt 1:2). And it could just as easily read, 'Jacob the father of Joseph who is one of Jacob's sons by his wife Rachel'. They share many experiences in common.

Both Josephs are pure in heart and in their actions and relationships. One Joseph refuses to be seduced by the wife of his Egyptian master and so goes to prison. The other Joseph will find himself in a compromising and difficult situation with Mary. Both are described as dreamers. In Genesis, Joseph's brothers cry out as he approaches them: 'Behold the dreamer cometh' (Gn 37:5-11). (It is not a compliment because his dreams are about power, homage and his place not only in their family but in their history to come.)

This is Joseph's annunciation story about the origins of the birth of Jesus and the invitation from God to be the father of his child.

> Now this is how the birth of Jesus Christ came about. When his mother Mary was engaged to Joseph but before they lived together, she was found with child through the power of the Holy Spirit. Joseph her husband, an upright man unwilling to expose her to the law, decided to divorce her quietly. Such was his intention when suddenly the angel of the Lord appeared in a dream and said to him: 'Joseph, son of David, have no fear about taking Mary as your wife. It is by the Holy Spirit that she has conceived this child. She is to have a son and you are to name him Jesus because he will save his people from their sins.' All this happened to fulfil what the Lord had said through the prophet: 'The virgin shall be with child and give birth to a son and they shall call him Emmanuel, a name which means "God is with us".'
>
> When Joseph awoke he did as the angel of the Lord had directed him and received her into his house as his wife. He had no relations with her at any time before she bore a son, whom he named Jesus. (Mt 1:18-25)

Most people react to this passage with questions about Joseph and dreams. They show disbelief and wonder at the way Joseph learns of the Incarnation and the presence of the Messiah in the world. They are stunned by how easily he adjusts his whole life to obey the angel's instruction. It doesn't make sense to most people today. However, this Joseph is not like most modern people, and Joseph is facing a dilemma. He is an upright and just man, obedient to the law, but he is also 'unwilling to expose her to the law' (the law found in Dt 22:23-24 and Nm 5:11-31, detailing why she should be 'stoned to death at the gate of the town').

Much of the background of Matthew's version of the Gospel specifically introduces violence both in the larger world of Rome and Israel and in the family and religion. It is steeped in Jewish tradition and practice but everything seems to expand and break out and away from established norms and practice. The genealogy includes the names of women who are gentile, involved in various odd circumstances many would label as sin and unholy: from prostitution (Tamar and Rehab), to murder (Bathsheba), and to outsiders who were enemies at the time of Israel (Ruth), ending with Mary. This begins with the reordering of history rather than the usual recording of one's ancestors.

Matthew's story is a jolt of reality, but his sobering account is closer to reality than the fantasy that has come to surround the birth of the poor child of God hidden in our midst.

The Feast of the Holy Innocents, the first martyrs, is celebrated only days after Christmas. Its proximity is like a shadow, a reminder of who this child is and how the places of power and military might react to him – then and now. It is a story about birth and death, unnecessary, brutal cold-blooded murder, mourning and weeping, and escape, for the time being. Yet Matthew's story is about hope, about the discovery of a promise coming true, about stars and wise men and those who journey looking for a future and wisdom. It is the story that acts as a bridge between the birth and all that is unknown of the youth and young adulthood of Jesus and John the Baptiser's appearance at the Jordan announcing repentance and the nearness of salvation and hope in the person of a Messiah. It is about beginnings. It carries hints of the adult man to come and foreshadows the rejection that will eventually overtake Jesus and draw him to his death on the cross.

The story begins immediately after the genealogy at the beginning of the Gospels. We begin here because it is also about the man Joseph, who is the father of Jesus, his protector, his security, his teacher, his link to his Jewish history and religious belief and practice. This is Joseph the dreamer who again and again stakes his life on dreams that are all connected to the child entrusted to him by God the Father. He must make sure the dreams become reality in his life and family and the child lives to be the Good News of God to the Poor. The child is born in Bethlehem of Judea during the reign of King Herod, appointed king by the Romans occupying the land. The scene has been set. Jesus is born of the house of David through Joseph, who is known as the husband of Mary, his earthly father.

What does it mean to be an upright or just Jew? It means strict adherence to the law and fidelity to the Word of God. Sometimes the elements of truthfulness, of care of the weak and the poor, of charity are included as well, along with giving others their due and considering the good of all. Rarely does anyone remember that justice can also be tender-hearted mercy, *hesed*, as in the descriptions of God's justice in the Hebrew scriptures. Joseph, being just and good, decides to divorce Mary or put her away quietly. The phrase 'put away' evokes overtones of hiding someone away, of brushing a situation under the rug, of covering up facts – much as many people would do if they found out that a woman was pregnant and unmarried, even today. Have the child, but send the mother away to a distant place, with cousins or to a home, hush it up and don't talk about what is really going on! Is this what Joseph has in mind?

Joseph does not want to have Mary executed, destroying both her and the child. If he divorces her quietly and separates himself from her, she and her child have a chance at life - but what kind of life? She would be a woman alone with a child, rejected, outcast; the child would be essentially fatherless, carrying the onus of illegitimacy forever. Still, it would be better than death. What did Joseph feel? Was he betrayed, broken-hearted, ashamed, rejected, hurt, angry, dejected, in despair? Remember, all his hopes and dreams of a life with Mary, of a future in the community, of happiness and the prospect of children and a family of his own are gone. All he can do is react or respond to the reality – Mary is with child and the child is not his child.

But Joseph like his namesake of old is a dreamer. And he sleeps and he dreams. The angel appears in his dream and tells him not to fear, to take Mary into his house as his wife because it is by the Holy Spirit that she has conceived a child. This is Gabriel who speaks of the Son of Man in the book of Daniel, who announces the future of Israel in history and what is to come. In the dream Gabriel calls him, Joseph, the son of David, the once great nation of kings, now long enslaved, but his lineage is that from whom the Promised One will come forth. Dreams are divine instructions that are intent on revealing history according to God and what is possible at this moment in time.

The dream is about the child, the saviour of his people, who forgives and sets them free. This child is the fulfilment of the hopes of the people of Israel, the divine presence of God with his people, the presence of justice, mercy and peace. Joseph awakes and obeys the command of the Lord. Joseph is a just Jew. He lives on the scriptures. In a sense, he eats, drinks, sleeps and dreams the Word of the Lord. He is steeped in the Law, the Prophets, the Psalms and the promises that Israel has lived on for generations.

John Sanford and many in the Jewish community refer to dreams as the forgotten language of God. Dreams, especially in Jewish understanding, are a way of communicating God's will to individuals that will directly impact the history of the people. Jewish people are willing to stake their life on the knowledge that is given in the dream, even though they are unable to explain to others why they act as they do. They dream, and the dream becomes knowledge born of hope, faith and belief in God. Joseph awakes and obeys the Word of God, and with the strength of the Spirit of God disregards the Law and takes Mary into his home as his wife and takes the child as his own. This is the wisdom of Joseph, born of his love and compassion for Mary and the child that is sourced in his deep understanding of the Law and the Prophets. He becomes the husband and the friend of Mary, the man who adopts God into his family; the protector of both, willing to shift his life toward hope, toward what this one child might become for his people.

Another parallel connection between the two Josephs is that 'both are fathers who are not fathers'. In the book of Genesis we read of Joseph taking with him his two sons, Manasseh and Ephraim, to see his father

Jacob who is ill and old. When he sees him, he summons his strength and sits up in bed and tells Joseph:

> God Almighty appeared to me at Luz in the land of Canaan, and he blessed me, and said to me, 'I am going to make you fruitful and increase your numbers; I will make of you a company of peoples, and will give this land to your offspring after you for a perpetual holding.' Therefore your two sons, who were born to you in the land of Egypt before I came to you in Egypt, are now mine; Ephraim and Manasseh shall be mine, just as Reuben and Simeon are. As for the offspring born to you after them, they shall be yours. They shall be recorded under the names of their brothers with regard to their inheritance.' (Gn 48:1-6)

Even though these two sons are listed in the twelve tribes of Israel as sons of Jacob, they are in fact, sons of Joseph. Joseph, the Jewish father of Jesus, is a father who is not a father. This is how it comes to be.

> In the Old Testament, nature is defied in an act of adopting. In the New Testament, it is God and not nature that makes Joseph the father of Jesus by instructing him to name the child Jesus (Mt 1:21). Naming a child is the father's role in the Bible. In fact, Joseph must be Jesus' father as it is through Joseph that Jesus 'the Messiah is the son of David, the son of Abraham' (Mt 1:1), the seed who will accomplish the promises made to both David and Abraham.[1]
>
> Joseph fulfils the role of a real father at every level … naming the child, becoming his protector in a hostile world (especially in the face of Herod's plots to destroy the child). Joseph is not the biological father but because of his faithfulness and his obedience he becomes the real father.[2]

This man Joseph is remarkable because of his graceful and spirit-filled response to a difficult and dangerous situation. He thinks first of those who are weaker and in danger; he sides with them, enduring much

---

1   Neuhaus, 'A Holy Family?', op. cit., pp. 33–5.
2   Neuhaus, 'Pastoral Letter', Saint James Vicariate for Hebrew-Speaking Catholics in Israel for 19 March, Feast of Saint Joseph (15 May 2017).

to honour their lives and their right to exist and to have a home. No wonder that Jesus' awareness of God as his father is filled with mercy, love, forgiveness, tenderness and compassion, care for the poor and the weak, endurance in the face of hardship and all events that seek to break that bond. His earthly father is a man of justice, an upright and holy man, a true child of God.

We think of another remarkable father, a teacher-father in many respects of the word. Here I quote the father of Malala Yousafzai.

> Before I became known as 'Malala's father', I worked as a teacher in Pakistan. It was not a well-respected occupation. In fact, a friend of my father said to me: 'We were expecting great things from you, Ziauddin. You could have been a political leader or a police chief, but instead you just became a teacher.'
>
> I told the man that if I inspired just one of the students in my class that year to be a leader, one again the next year, and one every year for the rest of my career, I would be very proud of my contribution to our community.
>
> I believe that educators are nation-builders. But too often our leaders ignore the role of teachers in creating good citizens, growing the economy, improving public health, and so much more. In most developing countries, teachers are untrained and poorly paid – and sometimes not paid at all.
>
> Our world needs to encourage, recruit and train more teachers. When trained educators lead a class, students stay in school longer and learn valuable critical thinking skills. That's why the Malala Fund supports organisations like Teach for Afghanistan, who work to recruit talented, motivated women graduates to help fill spots in Afghanistan's overcrowded classrooms.
>
> To me, being a teacher is the most rewarding profession. I hope that someday teachers will be as highly regarded as doctors, engineers and computer scientists.

What role does the Spirit play in all of this, in the conception of the child and in Joseph's awareness of the reality of who this child is? It seems from the rest of Chapter 1 of Matthew's Gospel, which include all the references we have to Joseph, that dreams will become the pattern of his life, the primary way that Joseph discerns what to do, when and why. Dreams are visions of reality that are able to encompass the personal details of people's lives and draw them into a new world of reality, to enable them to create a world when one does not yet exist, to include the loose and lost pieces that one grows to cherish and honour and love and wrap one's life around. Joseph, the dreamer par excellence, like his namesake in Genesis, dreams a better world, one that is more holy, more careful of the weak and the little ones, one that opens up possibilities of God's working among humankind in unbelievably kind ways. Joseph is like God: he believes in human beings and in life and in the promises given to his people over the ages. Like Mary, he is ready. He has been waiting all his life for the hope to be made manifest, for the Word of the Lord to once again interrupt history and reveal the power of the Lord.

Joseph believes that God is revealing himself in Mary and in his own life and that God is counselling him. Like any prophet of old, he obeys and life is radically altered forever. His dilemma is solved using the Scripture (quoted by Gabriel from the book of the prophet Isaiah), his own contemporary experience and knowledge, and he decides he must protect and sustain the life of all involved. This entails putting his own life, his honour and reputation in jeopardy and putting their honour and lives on a par with his own. The Spirit gives birth to Joseph in a new, creative, life-giving response of what to do in this situation. He too conceives by the power of the Holy Spirit, as surely as his wife Mary does.

Joseph is the shadow of the Father (in heaven) and he becomes the father of Jesus on earth. In listening to and obeying the Word of the Lord, he creates a possibility never dreamed of before. He acts in faith, radically converted to life, severs himself from rigid adherence to the Law and does justice for this woman, his wife, and their child. They become now every woman and child, the least, the poorest, those without power, or anyone specifically endangered by law, cult, tradition, society or institution. Joseph in Matthew's Gospel is the image of the catechumen for all those baptised into the community – every Jew that will become a Christian and all gentiles who must learn to move beyond or deeper into the law, into the Spirit, loving all, even enemies. Joseph is young, probably around fifteen, with Mary perhaps a bit younger, having become adult Jews at the age of twelve. He awakes (often a term used to refer to Baptism, the sacrament of Enlightenment) and obeys the Word of the Lord. A new way of being human is being born.

This family of Mary, with child and betrothed, and Joseph, a just and upright man who takes her in and cares for her and the child of God, is a new image of family – not bound by blood, or marriage, or sexual ties, but by the bonds of faith, of need, and of compassion that serves life. It reflects the kingdom and will of God, who fathers and births us all. It is Joseph who will hold this family together in the face of history's callousness and violence, Herod's fear and agitation and the hardships of being poor and Jewish in occupied territory that belongs to the harsh domination of the Romans.

This is the Holy Family: it began with Elizabeth and Zechariah and John who grew up to be the Baptiser who went before Jesus' face. Then it spread to Mary, betrothed to Joseph of Nazareth, then to poor shepherds in the fields of Bethlehem; then to Simeon and Anna, ancient faithful ones who will meet them in the temple when they come for circumcision and cleansing. And it is acknowledged first by strangers and gentiles from afar who will search for wisdom in the heavens, the skies and the stars, who seek the Child, and it will spiral out from there to all the earth.

WHEN TERROR SHADOWS THEM

The story that follows the birth of Jesus in Matthew's Gospel is what we call the slaughter of the innocents and the flight into Egypt. It is initiated by the decree of Herod to slay the children of Bethlehem. We are more at home with the story of Jesus' birth from Luke's Gospel, because it is the traditional one read at the Christmas Vigil liturgy. We envision angels singing 'Gloria' and simple shepherds going to Bethlehem to find the Child wrapped in swaddling clothes and lying in a manger attended by his mother and Joseph. It is the image of Christmas cards and greetings of peace on earth, the mother and child, serene though poor, full of awe and joy in the stable with the worshipping animals and Joseph standing off to the side.

The Feast of the Holy Innocents is celebrated only days after Christmas. Its proximity is like a shadow, a truthful reminder of who this child is and how the places of power and military might react to him

– then and now. It is a story about birth and death, unnecessary death, brutal cold-blooded murder, mourning and weeping, and escape, for the being. Yet Matthew's story is about hope, about the discovery of a promise coming true, about stars and wise ones and those who journey looking for the future and wisdom. It is the story that acts as a bridge between the birth and youth of Jesus and John the Baptiser's appearance at the Jordan announcing repentance and the nearness of salvation and hope in the person of the Messiah. It is about beginnings. It carries hints of the grown man to come and foreshadows the rejection that will eventually overtake Jesus and draw him to his death on the cross. The story begins forthrightly and is laced with an ominous overcast.

> After Jesus' birth in Bethlehem of Judea during the reign of King Herod, astrologers from the east arrived one day in Jerusalem inquiring, 'Where is the newborn king of the Jews? We observed his star at its rising and have come to pay him homage.' At this news King Herod became greatly disturbed, and with him all of Jerusalem. Summoning all of the chief priests and scribes of the people, he inquired of them where the Messiah was to be born. 'In Bethlehem of Judea,' they informed him. 'Here is what the prophet has written: "And you, Bethlehem, land of Judah, are by no means least among the princes of Judah, since from you shall come a ruler who is to shepherd my people Israel".' (Mt 2:1-6)

The child is named Joshua – Saviour – and his star is rising. Bethlehem is a small village outside the city of Jerusalem, and the prophecy combines Micah 5:1 and 2 Samuel 5:2. Matthew is interested in connecting Jesus to the Jewish traditions and prophecies because Matthew's community has been cast out from the Jewish life of faith and practice. This occurred because of the community's refusal to fight the Romans alongside the Jews in trying to save the Temple from destruction. Matthew's community is struggling for an identity that is not just Jewish but one that fulfils the hopes and words of the past and brings them fullness and insight for the present. Often Matthew's Gospel is interwoven with texts from the Hebrew scriptures that validate who Jesus is and suggest how Jesus not only fulfilled these texts but went beyond them. Matthew's community stakes its belief and practice on the extended spirit of the texts as revealed in the life and person and teaching of Jesus.

It seems that while the chief priests and scribes know where the Messiah is to be born, King Herod does not and it disturbs him greatly. And when the king is disturbed, the whole city is up in arms. Now Herod was known for erratic behaviour, for violence and intrigue and deception and ruthlessness, even among his own family. His power, his rule and his position as king in Jerusalem were his primary concerns. Nothing that threatened his position – even a child – was to be tolerated. Threats were dealt with quickly, politically or militarily.

The wise men, often referred to as kings but more likely scholars, arrive. They have knowledge of the hope and promises of the scriptures and also of the sky and heavens. They are searching, inquiring and so intent on finding and paying homage to this child that they are willing to leave their own lands and positions. They go to another country and approach its ruler for more precise information. They are seekers of God, of wisdom, astrologers who follow what the stars tell them. They are not so different from Joseph, who follows his dreams, or the people of Israel, who live on promises and the hope that God's promises will be kept in God's own time and in God's own ways – when the time is fulfilled and all is ready.

They share what they know with King Herod, who checks out their information with his own advisors (it is interesting to note that there are many scribes and chief priests of the people who seem to serve the king before they serve God or the people). These advisors verify the information of the outsiders who have come to Israel. The initial reaction to the good news of the presence of the Messiah is one of profound disturbance. Even the thought that there might be someone who would one day rule in his place angers Herod and moves him to action – to deceit and cunning. He will use the magi and their information to find out what he needs to know about this child and to ensure that there will be no threat to his reign.

> Herod called the astrologers aside and found out from them the exact time of the star's appearance. Then he sent them to Bethlehem, after having instructed them: 'Go and get detailed information about the

child. When you have found him, report it to me so that I may go and offer him homage too.' (Mt 2:7-8)

Herod plans to use the seekers – who are rather naive politically – to get the information he needs to destroy the child. He pretends he too is a good Jew, waiting for the one who will shepherd the people of God and bring the people hope and justice. He sends the magi on their way. Governments and those in power often lead their people to think one thing while actively plotting the exact opposite. They use the unsuspecting and unaware for their own destructive ends.

So, the astrologers leave the king and proceed on their way.

After their audience with the king, they set out. The star which they had observed at its rising went ahead of them until it came to a standstill over the place where the child was. They were overjoyed at seeing the star, and on entering the house, found the child with Mary his mother. They prostrated themselves and did him homage. Then they opened their coffers and presented him with gifts of gold, frankincense and myrrh. They received a message in a dream not to return to Herod, so they went back to their own country by another route. (Mt 2:9-12)

They are overjoyed to see the star – the star is their beacon, their lifeline to the future, their hope. The star comes to a standstill over the place where the child is. No wonder the newborn one is often referred to, in some cultures and among some storytellers, as the star child. They enter the house – in Matthew's Gospel, the house is the community of believers, the Church – and do the child homage.

They worship and open their coffers and present the child with gifts. The three gifts are the source of the belief that there were three wise men. Their gifts have come to symbolise the future and the hidden identity of the child. Gold represents his kingship; frankincense, his priesthood; and myrrh, his suffering as the servant of God. These are customary gifts in the Orient as signs of homage. They are the first signs and presences of people outside the Jewish community and Israel who recognise Jesus as Messiah and hope, not just for the Jews, but for all the nations of the world. In Matthew's Gospel it is the Gentiles who first acknowledge Jesus as saviour and who will later be the strength of the believing community, part of those shepherded and drawn into the fold.

These strangers are then given a dream, a message not to go back to Herod. They obey and go home by another route. An encounter with the child changes everything. They are given knowledge that now protects, rather than knowledge or information that can be used against the child and his family. The astrologers go home with more than just the sight of the child, their moment of adoration and worship. They go home as part of the promise, the future and the hope of God now present in the world. They are to become witnesses, those who proclaim to outsiders that the mercy of God is now present in the world for all who seek life and hope, all who follow the stars and use whatever knowledge and wisdom they have to serve God. They now have an inner star, a dream, the Spirit to lead them on their journey and throughout their life, back into their own countries and communities. The Spirit and the Word are spreading.

Then Joseph dreams again.

> After they had left, the angel of the Lord suddenly appeared in a dream to Joseph with the command: 'Get up, take the child and his mother, and flee to Egypt. Stay there until I tell you otherwise. Herod is searching for the child to destroy him.' Joseph got up and took the child and his mother and left that night for Egypt. He stayed there until the death of Herod, to fulfil what the Lord had said through the prophet: 'Out of Egypt I have called my son.' (Mt 2:13-15)

The dream is imperious: 'suddenly', 'get up', 'flee', 'stay there'. Joseph's response is immediate and unquestioning: he left that very night. They stay in Egypt, awaiting another dream, another angel, another word from the Lord. There is an echo of the prophets here: the Word of the Lord comes and obedience is swift and uncompromising. Joseph probably knew that the astrologers had told Herod about their journey and search for the child. Joseph is not naive about the wrath and hate that drive Herod. His awareness and his faith together combine to unconsciously warn him, and the angel – the message of God – is heeded. The child, the mother and Joseph become sojourners in Egypt, illegal aliens, foreigners in a strange land where they remain hidden until word comes to Egypt of the death of Herod. The angel then returns to announce that it is safe to go back. In Matthew's Gospel Jesus echoes Moses, David and the prophets. His family sojourns in Egypt and then returns to the land of Israel. The child grows up to be the greatest teacher and prophet and king ever seen in Israel's history.

Joseph descends into Egypt like his namesake of old in Genesis. Joseph will save his brothers and his father from starvation and rescue his kin from famine – Joseph has dreamed of the years of plenty and the years of hunger. Now Joseph and his family are threatened with death from Herod, and Egypt becomes a place of safety for the family. They will hide there, yet they will also depart from there to return to Israel as the Israelites left Egypt for the promised land.

And now comes the torn, tragic heart of the story.

> Once Herod realised that he had been deceived by the astrologers, he became furious. He ordered the massacre of all the boys two years old and under in Bethlehem and its environs, making his calculations on the basis of the date he had learned from the astrologers. What was said through Jeremiah the prophet was then fulfilled: 'A cry was heard at Ramah, sobbing and loud lamentation: Rachel bewailing her children; no comfort for her, since they are no more.' (Mt 2:16-18)

These few lines recount destruction and murder, the slaughter of the innocents, the loss not only of their children but of hope and life for countless women and men. The massacre is a brutal reminder of the reaction of power to anything that potentially threatens its rule. There is no refuge for those unsuspectingly caught in the web of hate and politics. One child is concealed and saved; others are exposed and murdered. The entire quotation from the prophet Jeremiah broadens our understanding about why this passage is included in Matthew's Gospel:

> Thus says the Lord: 'In Ramah is heard the sound of mourning, of bitter weeping! Rachel mourns her children, she refuses to be consoled because her children are no more.' Thus says the Lord: 'Cease your cries of mourning, wipe the tears from your eyes, the sorrow you have shown shall have its reward, says the Lord; they shall return from the

enemy's land. There is hope for your future, says the Lord; your sons shall return to their own borders.' (Jer 31:15-17)

Ramah is a small village north of Jerusalem, the traditional burial place of Rachel, whose children and grandchildren were the descendants of Ephraim, chief of the northern tribes, the exiles from Jerusalem. Along with the destruction comes hope: God will remember, will answer and will bring them back. There will be a new people, a new covenant, a new promise that encompasses the old and goes far beyond it. God remains with his people, especially in their suffering and death.

And yet the destruction, the loss of the children, the slaughter of the innocents, the brutality of the ruler, the ruthless response of power and killing are also remembered. Matthew sounds an early warning: any kind of association with this man Jesus, even when he is a helpless child, can be dangerous because of the hope he brings to earth. This is a hope that will undo injustice and overthrow those who do not serve God but rather their own kingdoms, who live not by forgiveness and care for the poor and the service of the people but by violence and selfishness, greed and power. This child, this man, is dangerous. Any kind of closeness to this child can be fatal.

The slaughter of the innocents and the fear of what might befall grown children is still with us. The hope of the future, of the kingdom of peace and justice, lies in the birth of any child, especially any child born to believers who struggle for justice and peace for all their brothers and sisters of the world.

The rest of this chapter of Matthew reveals little of the life of Jesus, Mary and Joseph until Jesus is grown and appears before John the prophet to be baptised.

> But after Herod's death, the angel of the Lord appeared in a dream to Joseph in Egypt with the command: 'Get up, take the child and his mother, and set out for the land of Israel. Those who had designs on the life of the child are dead.' He got up, took the child and his mother, and returned to the land of Israel. He heard, however, that Archelaus had succeeded his father Herod as king of Judea, and he was afraid to go back there. Instead, because of a warning received in

a dream, Joseph went to the region of Galilee. There he settled in a
town called Nazareth. In this way, what was said through the prophets
was fulfilled: 'He shall be called a Nazorean.' (Mt 2:19-23)

The family stays in Egypt until the political situation shifts. This child,
who will influence the course of history so strongly, lives in its shadow
from the beginning. The dreams come when they are needed. The Spirit
is with Joseph whenever he must make decisions and act for the benefit
of the child and his mother. Joseph's care is for his family. His daylight
fears and knowledge of what is going on in Judea and Jerusalem point
him towards Nazareth, a nowhere town of both Jews and Gentiles. There
Jesus grows up.

> To say that Jesus is a Messiah-Nazarene is equivalent to saying that
> Jesus is a Messiah-*severino*, that is a messiah who assumes the severity
> of life and death *severina*, the hard life of anonymous people, those
> anonymous people who are called in the northeast of Brazil, *severinos*.
>   … God, however, wanted to incarnate exactly in this situation the
> 'Nazarene', that is, *severina*, the humble and contradictory. In other
> words, God revealed himself in Jesus not because Jesus is 'human', but
> because Jesus is 'Nazarene', which is the same as saying because Jesus
> is poor, despised, simple and unknown just as the *severinos* of history.[3]

Joseph, Mary and Jesus settle in Nazareth; they live unhindered, unknown,
and so in safety, while the political and economic realities of Israel, an
occupied territory with a brutal Jewish king, remain the same. The family
of Joseph, that just and upright man, and his wife, Mary, and the child
Jesus, who was once saved from murder, disappears for thirty years.
Nothing is known except that Jesus is a Jew, taught and nurtured by Jewish
parents who are just and live on the Word of the Lord and believe in the
dreams of God for the people. Jesus is formed by this man and woman
and the historical realities, brutal memories, the promises of the scriptures
and the Spirit, who conceived him and has been friend to his parents,
and those who see him for who he truly is – the one who will save his
people from their sins and the sins of the nation.

---

3 Boff, *Saint Joseph*, op. cit., pp. 41–2.

Amazingly, as Boff has it, 'If Mary gave to Jesus the physical "flesh", it was Joseph who provided the "*severina* flesh", the historic-social condition of poverty, by deciding to live in Nazareth.'[4]

This story is outrageous, full of the danger, deceit, unwarranted brutality, insensitivity and horror that unfortunately form the daily life of many in the human race, both then and today. The cruelty of the world, of governments and nations and individuals, is part of the Christmas story. It must be remembered and told. Jesus was born among the poor and massacred innocents of history. The cynical and cowardly eyes of those in political systems see the birth of such children as insignificant. But our belief is that God became human through just such an 'insignificant' event and dwelled among us, and still dwells among us. God entered history and has stayed in it. God became human in the flesh of the poor, the masses of people forgotten by society's institutions and governments. God burst into history in a very unlikely time and place with very ordinary parents. His home was a place occupied by military troops, with a puppet king, in the midst of repression and oppression.

Jesus is born among people who endure. God is born in solidarity with the poor and the slaughtered innocents. By the choice of time and place and the historical circumstances of his birth and presence, God, in the person of Jesus, is the first human to make an option for the poor. His very presence evokes fear, death and reprisals – immediate and brutal. This cannot be ignored; it has been the tradition and memory of the Church since Matthew's community.

Liturgically we celebrate these first martyrs, caught in the web of hatred of God's presence and hope, on 28 December, just three days after the birth of the star child. The birth of hope among the poor may not seem important to many of us, but those in power know and sense that it means the end of their reign of hate and injustice. The joy of Christmas and its serenity and hope are shattered by tragedy and the shared horror of loss and massacre. The events cast a long shadow, one reaching to a cross.

Rachel wept and would not be comforted, for her children were no more. Rachel still weeps in every country of the world – in the last decades in El Salvador, Guatemala, Haiti, Peru and Northern Ireland. Today there are staggering new names to the litany of countries devastated by war that

---

4 Ibid.

drives millions of people from their homes. Still Palestine and the West Bank remain on the list, joined by at least a million or more children (not counting their parents) from Syria, many of the countries of the Middle East and Eritrea.

The United Nations Agency reported in July 2017 on the numbers of displaced people in the world. The statistics are hard to connect to the reality that each number is a living, breathing human person. Here are the numbers:

There are 65.6 million displaced people in the world – more people than the number that live in the United Kingdom.

22.5 million are refugees.

40.3 million are displaced in their own country.

2.8 million are seeking asylum.

Where do they come from? Syria: 5.5 million (almost 2 million of these are children); Afghanistan: 2.5 million; South Sudan: 1.4 million.

Equally revealing are those countries who are receiving the refugees: Turkey: 2.9 million; Pakistan: 1.4 million; Lebanon: 1 million; Iran: 979,400; Uganda: 940,800; Ethiopia: 791,600.

The poor are taking in those poorer still: those reduced to sheer human misery and survival. There are those who flee into exile, sojourn in foreign lands and live in daily fear of reprisals and exposure. They carry a memory of horror and pain for others who do not escape from war, from genocide, from starvation and famine, from slaughter between nations intent on their own violent agenda. Still the innocent are caught and suffer terribly. Peace on earth is a dream for the poor and for children who have never known peace. They live a dangerous existence, but they know the child of peace born among them, the one who ultimately sealed their births and hopes with the blood and sacrifice of the cross, the light to the nations and a judgement on all the earth.

The epiphany, the manifestation and showing forth of God, reminds us all that God dwells hidden among us and that the poor and the innocent massacred in history are the star that rises now in the new covenant. This child of hope is a universal child, a universal wisdom of peace with justice and care for the poor. This is where each of us is confronted with a choice – to remain in the history of violence and war and insensitivity to the poor, or to go home by another route and choose the wisdom of the cross and the star and the poor child of God. The Gospel story is a warning for us to remember how history treats the poor and the oppressed and those who side with them, and it is also a song of hope for how God feels about these people and their unending belief in a time of justice and mercy and life lived in grace and peace. Birth and the crime against the birth of hope are tied together at Christmas. The Word of the Lord can instill a song that overjoys the heart, or it can disturb an entire nation, unsettling the status quo and threatening systems of injustice and violence. The innocents, the holy ones, are murdered; only a few escape, haunted by the memory of death. The martyrs who are infants, children, the old, the women and men who live with the slaughter and the wrenching in their hearts and souls are many. Their number increases down to the present.

Scientists say today that everything on earth, every molecule of matter, even every atom of our bodies is matter that was once a star. We are made of stars and dreams and the Word of the Lord. Once we know that, encounter that – in the scriptures, in the poor, in the slaughter of the innocents – there is only one graced response: we have to go home by another route, by the way of Jesus, the way of hope for the poor, the way of blood and truth, the way of the cross. Another Herod helped to kill Jesus, but the dream rose joyfully, destroying death. The dream rises in every child born, in every response in faith to the Word of the Lord, in every encounter with the poor, in every act of homage and worship that gifts those in need, in every radical act of disobedience, and in every resistance to any power that is not based on the power of the one who is Jesus, Joshua, the one who saves us from our sins and calls us to be star children, the children of Mary and Joseph, the children of God. Christmas, the birth of grace and spirit, is today, here in all of us.

The story continues today. It is our story now: our history and geography, our religious belief and dreams as Christians in the world of nearly eight billion people. It convicts us, questions us, challenges us, dares us to live like Joseph making the dreams of God come true in our decisions, choices and daily devotion to our families and our extended families, all the beloved children of God. Meister Eckhart centuries ago put it this way: 'We are celebrating the feast of the Eternal Birth which God the Father has borne and never ceases to bear in all eternity. But if it takes not place in me, what avails it? Everything lies in this, that it should take place in me.' Now this birth must take place in us.

Prayer For Refugees
Sheltering God,
You were born in flight.
Your parents anxious and given no rest.
The manner of Your birth calls us to
Open-heartedness and sensitivity to the strangers in our midst.
Help us not to flee Your challenge.
The violence of the present time teaches us fear of the stranger,
Reluctant to reach out to those who are different.
Grace us this day as we seek
To see You in the faces of those uprooted,
Weary, as they seek refuge and peace. Amen.

(Jane Deren, Education for Justice)

Chapter 5
The Night of Birth

WHAT CHILD IS THIS?

Mary and Joseph's role in the Incarnation, the mystery of God becoming human flesh, is only two lines in the account of the birth of Jesus: 'They were in Bethlehem when the time came for her to have her child, and she gave birth to a son, her firstborn. She wrapped him in swaddling clothes and laid him in the manger, because there was no place for them in the inn' (Lk 2:6-7).

She delivers her child away from home and relatives, away from security and familiarity. She is on her way in obedience to the state, to be counted in a census as a member of an oppressed people in the occupied territory of another empire. She gives birth alone, with Joseph as midwife, in a place where animals shelter from the cold. She has very little to offer her firstborn, just her life and love. She is like every other poor woman who gives birth in a world that is alien and threatening, divided into nations, races and kingdoms.

But there have been strange things since the beginning of her pregnancy that happen all around her. She is told to go and visit her kinswoman Elizabeth, barren all her life, now old, yet pregnant. The strange wondrous event of Elizabeth and Zechariah's announcement of their child so late in life has been noted by their neighbours. His conception after the experience of Zechariah being struck dumb in the temple when he is given the news and his doubt, then the baby's birth and the naming ceremony, are premonitions of what is to come in Jesus' birth. When it is time to name the child as was the Jewish custom, they all assumed he would be named after his father but it is Elizabeth, his mother, who says:

'No, he is to be called John.' They said to her, 'None of your relatives has this name.' Then they began motioning to his father to find out what name he wanted to give him. He asked for a writing tablet and wrote, 'His name is John.' And all of them were amazed. Immediately his mouth was opened and his tongue freed, and he began to speak, praising God. Fear came over all their neighbours, and all these things were talked about throughout the hill country of Judea. All who heard them pondered them and said, 'What then will this child become?' For, indeed the hand of the Lord was with him. (Lk 1:60-66)

The naming of this child 'John' looses the tongue of his father. And as Mary the prophet sings with Elizabeth, now Zechariah sings of the blessings and praises of God.

And you, child, will be called the prophet of the Most High; for you will go before the Lord to prepare his ways, to give knowledge of salvation to his people by the forgiveness of their sins. By the tender mercy of our God, the dawn from on high will break upon us, to give light to those who sit in darkness and in the shadow of death, to guide our feet in the way of peace.(Lk 1:76-79)

These thoughts will be echoed by many who become aware of the birth of this child born to Joseph and Mary.

The birth does not go unnoticed. The small family is visited by poor shepherds who come looking for the Messiah. After Mary and Elizabeth and the child John leaping and dancing in Elizabeth's womb, the first to hear the good news of peace coming to earth in the person of God are shepherds, people of no worth. Gabriel, this time accompanied by heavenly choirs, comes to Bethlehem and glory descends upon the lowly and the meek.

In El Salvador refugees flee the government troops, hiding in the jungle only a couple of thousand yards away from the troops that would kill them. The group stops long enough for a woman to give birth, in devastating silence and pain. The women around her hold her, willing her to make no sound. The child, once born, is passed from hand to hand, blessed, prayed over. Each person hopes that this child will be the one that will help to free the people and bring peace to their land. Then they move on, with new life to be celebrated at the first stop where it is safe to sing, to rejoice, to eat together, and give blessings to the mother.

Today this experience continues with the nearly two million people and their women giving birth on the road, wherever they can stop, as they flee their homelands in countries like South Sudan, Somalia, Nigeria and Kenya in Africa, and in Syria, Palestine and Yemen in the Middle East. Mary's child likewise was born into a world that was hostile and fearful of the children of the poor, especially Jewish children. Women of war-torn countries birth their children with Mary, intent on giving life to the earth in the face of hate, war and death. The poor, the farmers, the peasants and other refugees wait in hope for this child to grow up.

The text points us only to the child. The traditional Christmas carol repeats the question: 'What child is this that lies sleeping on Mary's lap?' The good news is about the birth of this child, the Son of God. That is the miracle that the angels herald and announce to poor folk. The words are clear:

'Don't be afraid: I am here to give you good news, great joy for all the peoples. Today a Saviour has been born to you in David's town; he is the Messiah and the Lord. Let this be a sign to you: you will find a baby wrapped in swaddling clothes and lying in a manger... Glory to God in the highest: peace on earth for God is blessing humankind.' (Lk 2:10-13)

A Blackfoot Indian story, told among a number of Indian tribes in the northern Midwest US, echoes this Christmas story. I first heard it from Ken Feit, an itinerant storyteller and shaman who was killed in a hit-and-run accident.

It was a long, long time ago. I was young then. You know I was a warrior and a scout for our people. It was winter, brutally cold and hard. There was little food, and everyone was hungry. The snow was deep and we went looking for our enemies. I was proud to be sent out. I travelled three days and three nights, running swiftly, searching for the winter camp of our enemies, the Crow.

On the third night I found a lone tepee in the forest. That is the way our enemies camped, scattered throughout the forest. In the event of an attack, they would scatter, but later they would all come together at a prearranged place. I knew I had found them, and my heart rejoiced.

I crept up close to the tepee. There was a rent in the tepee, so I went down on my knees so I could see in through the ragged tear. I saw a young couple, no more than twenty, talking intently at a fire. A young child, no more than two, was playing nearby. He would stand on his wobbly legs and with a large wooden spoon stir the soup pot on the fire. He was imitating what he had seen his elders do: he would stir the soup, blow on the spoon, taste it, and then stir it again. And then, suddenly, he looked straight at me. He was on eye level with me! He saw me spying on them. I was afraid. But then, he put the spoon in the pot and filled it with soup and walked on his stubby little legs over toward me and fed me soup, through the tent flap!

I was taken aback – his parents would surely notice. But they were intent on their talk and were not paying any attention to the child at play. And the child waddled back toward the fire and repeated his little ritual. Again and again he came back to the tear in the tepee and fed me soup. Finally I slipped away, running in the night back toward my camp. I knew where the enemy camp was and must tell my people. We would catch them unawares and kill them, as they had done to us years ago. I ran and ran and ran.

Finally I could run no more. I sat on a great stone in the woods, pondering what I had seen and what had happened to me. It was the child. What child was this? What child would fearlessly feed an enemy soup with a wooden spoon through a tear in a tent flap? What power or Spirit protected this child and taught it its own ways? The child must live. What was I to do? I thought of going back and killing the parents and taking the child myself, to raise him in our tribe's ways and wisdom. But no, the child was too young; he needed his own parents and his people's ways. Finally, I knew what I had to do.

I returned to the tepee, and even though I was painted for war, I entered through the front of the tepee. The young couple was frightened, but I gave the signs of peace and was welcomed and seated at the fire. While the father prepared the peace pipe and the woman fidgeted, the young child smiled broadly in recognition. Once again the ritual was enacted: the child stirred the soup pot, blew on the spoon, tasted it, and waddled over to me and fed me the soup. The woman was astounded, but I spoke in signs and told them that it was the child who would save their lives this night. We spoke and ate, and I told them I had to return to my people and give them the information on this winter camp. But I would spare their lives because of the child's hospitality and love of enemy. They must leave when I left, taking only what they could carry on their backs, telling no one what happened. I watched them go with only a few possessions. The last thing I saw was the young father and mother running and on the woman's back was the child, waving the soup spoon in his hand and smiling at me still.

I returned quickly to my people and within days we attacked the camp of the enemy. It wasn't a battle, it was a slaughter. That was many, many winters ago. But I often have thought about that child. What child was that? What power and great Spirit protected him? What would this child grow up to be? Whenever I was in trouble and dismayed, I prayed to the Spirit that protected that child, and always I was cared for and protected as well. That child now will be grown to a man, a man of peace, kindness and hospitality. I wonder where he is and what he is about. For since that night, I have left the old ways of the warrior and scout and become your holy man. I lost my taste for war in the taste of the child's soup. Nothing has been the same since that night of being fed the Great Spirit's food at the hand of the unknown child. All I know now is that we need that child grown to manhood. We all need that child of peace among us now.

The night of Christmas belongs to the babe born in the place of sheep and lambs, wrapped in swaddling cloths, welcomed into the world by shepherds and animals. What child is this? In the ancient words of Isaiah, this child 'breaks the yoke of our burden, the bar across our shoulders, the rod of the oppressors, and this child rules in peace, and there will be no end to it. Justice and righteousness we will know from this time onward and forever' (Is 9:3, 6). This child, this baby is the heart of God in our flesh, the heart of the universe and each of our hearts. It is the mystery of God becoming flesh of our flesh. This is where we begin to understand that we follow the one who opted for the lost, the losers, the children of the world, the forsaken and the anonymous, the expendable, the ones in the fields.

This is God's solidarity with the earth. This is Bethlehem's starry night and the secret that the poor have long awaited. This is prelude to Calvary's harsh daylight execution and the wood of the cross. Feeding trough and hard bed and board – the legacy of so many of God's children. As the shepherds are summoned to the manger and the swaddled child, we are summoned to the presence of the poor. The glory of God declares for all the world to hear that God is not with the rulers of the world. God is outside, with those who find no room inside, who often find no room with us either.

Bethlehem is still disputed territory in the West Bank, and everywhere the poor of God huddle and wait for safety, for aid, for hope as other human beings decide whether people are worth caring for or worth intervening for on their behalf. Christmas theology sings lullabies to the child of God born to us who makes all people of the universe the beloved daughters and sons of God. All are our relatives, born of one flesh and of God's great heart. The cry of Mary and Joseph's child is a divine cry for justice and a cry of liberation for all. It is the cry of God praying that we will remember why all of us and creation were made: we were made for love alone!

In both the accounts in Luke and Matthew, it is about the child: poor, a source of distress, the one who will choose good and refuse evil; born under threat, in secret among ponderings and anguish; in oppression, occupied territory, being counted like the animals; whose presence triggers hard decisions for everyone, in the midst of violence that is directed first at him and then at those around him. But this child's birth also brings holiness and hope just by his coming into the world as the presence of God the Word made flesh among us. That Word must be born in us, more powerfully than he was born in history centuries ago. This is the mystery of the Incarnation that continues in the present, now for all time.

It is the birth of the Word that is Truth, Light and Peace: words that are almost interchangeable in the scriptures, as all of us are born as a child who opens up a space in the world that expands into a refuge, a sanctuary, a hospice, holy ground, a secure place build on justice for all. His name is Peace. There is a crack in the universe that starts in Nazareth, and it begins to grow in Bethlehem, then Egypt. It is God's glory revealed in the poor that we now call the Good News of God that will bring forth hope and challenge all human beings. His name is Mercy. 'He has granted mercy in the abundance of steadfast love' (Is 63:7-9). And this is Mercy that disturbs power. Reactions and responses to this child's presence in the world begin almost immediately.

Chapter 6
The Marriage of Joseph and Mary:
Husband and Wife; Friends and Disciples

THE SHADOW OF THE SWORD AND THE WORD

The child is born and Joseph and Mary now begin their lives together as family, as husband and wife, and parents in society. We do not know how long their life together as a married couple lasted. We only have two stories, both in Luke's Gospel, where they are seen together in public as family. The first story has them bringing their child to the temple, obeying the laws of purification and then giving back to God their firstborn son in the rite of circumcision. This is the story that has traditionally been called the Presentation. But the story is an amalgam of obedience to two separate commandments in the Jewish faith. The rite of circumcision would have taken place eight days after the birth while the experience that is called the Presentation is both the thirty-day redemption of the first born and the forty-day purification of a woman who has borne a son. They offer and consecrate their child to God's will and work, making him holy unto the Lord on behalf of his people.

Marriage is a universal institution, though practiced in as many ways as there are cultures and religion, which evolve and change over history. *Amoris Laetitia* begins with this definition:

> As a social institution, marriage protects and shapes a shared commitment to deeper growth in love and commitment to one another for the good of society as a whole. That is why marriage is more than a fleeting fashion; it is of enduring importance. Its essence derives from our human nature and social character. It involves a series of obligations born of love itself, a love so serious and generous that it is ready to face any risk.[1]

This is the sort of marriage that Joseph commits himself to when he takes Mary into his house as his wife, according to the traditions of Jewish

---

1 AL, 131.

betrothal. His option 'for marriage in this way expresses a genuine and firm decision to join paths, come what may. Given its seriousness, this public commitment of love cannot be the fruit of a hasty decision, but neither can it be postponed indefinitely. Committing oneself exclusively and definitively to another person always involves a risk and a bold gamble'.[2]

Joseph and Mary begin their life together after the birth of Jesus, attending to the rituals of obligation regarding the shift in their relations as they become parents. The family goes to the city of Jerusalem to offer two turtledoves or pigeons, as was the custom among the poor. When they enter the Temple's outer courtyards, they meet a number of people. First is Simeon.

> There lived in Jerusalem at this time a very upright and devout man named Simeon; the Holy Spirit was in him … He had been assured by the Holy Spirit that he would not die before seeing the Messiah of the Lord. So he was led into the Temple by the Holy Spirit at the time when the parents brought the child Jesus, to do for him according to the custom of the Law. Simeon took the child in his arms and blessed God, saying:
>
> 'Now, O Lord, you can dismiss your servant in peace, for you have fulfilled your word and my eyes have seen your salvation, which you display for all the people to see. Here is the light you will reveal to the nations and the glory of your people Israel.' (Lk 2:25-32)

The Spirit sends Simeon into the Temple to meet Mary and Joseph and the child. Simeon is filled with the Holy Spirit. He is part of the remnant of the holy people of Israel, waiting in hope for salvation and justice. He is faithful and true, waiting on the Word of the Lord told in the prophets. As the young family enters the Temple, he enters also. This story is the reading for the Feast of the Holy Family, the Sunday after Christmas. It reveals what family looks like in the kingdom, the kingdom of this child. Simeon is an old man who is sure that he will not die before seeing salvation in the midst of the people. He takes the child in his arms and blesses God with joy, delight and great comfort. He is not just intent on seeing the child for himself but on behalf of all the people. He recognises the light

2   Ibid., 132.

in the child, the light of the world, the hope of the future, the fulfilment of the promises. God's Word has come true in the presence of this child.

We know little of Simeon, 'the receiver of God', only that he is 'righteous and devout, looking forward to the consolation of Israel and the Holy Spirit rested on him' (Lk 2:25). There is a Christian midrash about him (compliments of the Jerusalem community of the Saint James Vicariate) that he was originally from Egypt and one of the seventy sages who were assembled by the King (around 285–246 BC) to translate the Jewish Bible into Greek (what we call the Septuagint). While he was translating he came across the line from Isaiah 7:14 that reads: 'Look, the virgin is with child and shall bear a son, and shall name him Emmanuel.' But he was plagued with doubt and decided there was an error in the text. He therefore decided to translate the word 'virgin' as 'woman'. But suddenly an angel of the Lord appeared to him, stopping his hand – much like the angel stopping the hand of Abraham obeying the command to sacrifice Isaac – and he was told: 'Believe what is written and you will see it accomplished; you will not die until you see the one who will be born of a virgin – the Messiah of the Lord.' And so Simeon lived for the prophecy to be fulfilled. It is said he waited long and that he was 360 years old when he was guided by the Spirit and arrives in the temple at the same time as Joseph, Mary and the child. Simeon is an elder, a grandparent in the family of Jesus, bound by belief in the scriptures, as so many of those who have gone before us in faith are to us. Our families in the Body of Christ are peopled by many who are not tied to us by blood or marriage but by belief and the Spirit's overshadowing. Legend has it that he died soon after and his bones are buried in the Church of Saint James.

We know that this is legend, but tradition connects us to our heritage and pasts, reminding us that our families and our faith is born of many others' faithfulness before us and that we are much more closely connected than we are often aware. And so there is another tradition that Simeon was the son of Hillel and the father of Gamaliel, the same man at whose feet Saul of Tarsus, the future apostle Paul, received his training and formation (cf. Acts 22:30). But the crucial description is always that Simeon had grown old, waiting like so many others for the one who would be 'the consolation of Israel'.

Simeon blesses the child. The image is one of an old man lifting the
child high above his head and offering him to God in sacrifice and singing
aloud. What must Mary and Joseph have thought! More for Mary to
ponder and treasure in her heart, marvelling at those who come to honour
her child. Then Simeon turns and addresses her, singling her out, apart
from Joseph.

> Then Simeon blessed them and said to his mother Mary, '[Behold]
> See him: for the multitudes of Israel he will be for their rise or their
> fall. He shall stand as a sign of contradiction, while a sword will pierce
> your own soul. Then the secret thoughts of everyone will be brought
> to light.' (Lk 2:34-35)

Does Simeon still hold the child while he tells Mary to look at Jesus and
see the child apart from herself, as mother? Can she see the child as part
of a people's history, in broad and far-reaching terms? This child is a child
of promise, and others, many others, will rise and fall in relation to him:
power, governments, religion, the poor. All must reckon with this child's
presence in the world. No one will go untouched. He stands as a sign of
contradiction, contradicting power, contradicting thoughts of good and
evil, contradicting what is true, what is law, what is just and unjust, what
is religious and holy, what is evil and sin. Again, all the focus is on the
child. Her child does not belong to her but to the people. This moment
begins to build on the experience of the shepherds' story when they come
to visit on the night of his birth. She must look at this child as more than
or other than her child. Her place, her part in the child's life? – in all of
this? – a sword will pierce her heart.

In Luke, Jesus comes to the Temple and is recognised by the Temple,
the seat of religious power and authority, but he is accepted and blessed
by unorthodox people, the people of the remnant of believers, those
who speak for the people themselves rather than those in the authority
structure of the Temple. The authority of the Spirit resides in the faithful
who rejoice at his presence and his obedience to the law.

The rite of circumcision reminded every Jewish couple that their
child was entrusted to them for care and protection but did not belong
to them. Each child was God's alone. The backdrop images are those of

Abraham and Isaac, and the binding of Abraham's descendants to God in the ritual of handing over and trusting God. The animals or birds are sacrificed in place of the child.

Jesus comes to the Temple as an Israelite, a believer in the promises. He will come again as teacher, as a young Jew coming of age, and he will come as prophet and Suffering Servant, willingly laying down his life and entrusting his body as sacrifice to God in obedience. From the beginning Jesus is the Suffering Servant, and all those bound to him share in that sacrifice and take part in his sufferings. In Luke, the shadow of the cross looms over all those bound to this child. This ritual of handing over to the Lord calls the parents to let go of their child. Simeon calls these parents to let go because this child belongs to all the nations more than he belongs to them.

From the beginning Mary and Joseph, as disciples, are reminded of the presence of the cross and the danger that this child's presence evokes. This is a warning, a shadow that hangs over their lives and the lives of all Christians, the followers of the light. We are saved in the shadow of the cross. This child will contradict everyone and evoke responses of anger, hate, discomfort, anxiety, loss and resistance. And while all this is happening to her child, the sword will enter Mary, pierce her. The conflict, violence and dislocation her child causes will have massive ramifications on her life and belief.

The sword of pain, penetration, intense suffering and struggle – and most important, the two-edged sword of the scriptures – will pierce Mary's heart and soul, both in blessing and pain. The Word of the Lord cuts straight through everyone's life: his disciples, friends and all who hear his preaching and reject, ignore, or come to belief. The sword in the upside-down position is the cross of the Suffering Servant that pierces Mary's life. From the very beginning in this Temple visit, the shadow is there. This child's body will be the new temple: the broken body of God on the cross that saves and welcomes all within its heart. Mary lives at the foot of the cross all her life and is marked from the beginning by the sign of the cross. The experience of violence against the innocent, the experience of injustice and its victims, the experience of non-violent resistance to evil is the experience of the Word and the cross in the life of all Christians.

'Then the secret thoughts of everyone will be brought to light.' The effect of contradiction and the cross is to reveal what is hidden from the light. Mary and all believers are intimately connected to this work of salvation. She is the silent witness to what transpires in her child's flesh and blood. We are witnesses, as followers of the light, to injustice, unnecessary suffering, violence and cold-blooded death. Our position as Christians is to stand by those who are the victims of the brutal inhumanity that is part of our world. This is Mary's call to discipleship as well: to pick up her cross and follow the man who is her master and Lord. The Word of the Lord and the cross of Christ are the same – a two-edged sword that reveals and purifies and saves.

Luke's Mary is the servant of the Suffering Servant, her child. The dreams she and Joseph have for their child must be laid aside for the dreams of the nations, the dreams of God. Even the sense of whom the child belongs to, and who belongs to his family, must be expanded and the boundaries pushed out to include the remnant of Israel: the widows, the orphans, the poor, those who carry the hidden Spirit, the faithful ones. In his family, blood ties, race, nation and gender are not important. What is crucial is belief, shared suffering and need. Soon this intimation of radical bonds of belief is made clear.

> Then his mother and his brothers came to him, but they could not get to him because of the crowd. Someone told him, 'Your mother and your brothers are standing outside and wish to meet you.' Then Jesus answered, 'My mother and my brothers are those who hear the word of God and do it.' (Lk 8:19-21)

This reference is found in Mark 3:31 and Matthew 12:46 even more clearly. There Jesus looks around at his disciples and says: 'Here are my mother and my brothers. Whoever does the will of God is brother and sister and mother to me.' Belief and practice of God's will are what create the bonds of community and family. Intimacy does not come primarily by family ties, marriage, race, or nation but through the Spirit.

We become kin to Jesus in our obedience to the Word and will of God, sharing the same passion and relationship that Jesus has with his God-Father. Mary and Joseph are the disciples and followers of this child of God, and our lives must resemble theirs in the struggle to believe and to expand the boundaries of our own communities and families. In this community, water is thicker than blood. The waters of Baptism draw us into the family. The blood ties that matter are the blood of the Eucharist, the blood of the cross, the blood of martyrs and the blood of reconciliation. If we want the intimacy that Mary had with her child, we can have it – by believing and obeying the will of God, as she did.

Mary is not allowed to keep her child for herself. She must grow into the awareness that this relationship is not special to her alone but belongs to anyone with whom God chooses to share it – those who hear the Word of God and let the sword pierce their own soul. At the cross, the place where the Word saves and the sword penetrates, we see who is mother, brother and sister to Jesus, the Son of God.

In Luke's account of the crucifixion, no one is at the foot of the cross when he dies. There are some who watch from a distance: 'Those who knew Jesus stood at a distance, especially the women who had followed him from Galilee; they witnessed all this' (Lk 23:49). It is this group of women who follow his body to the tomb, intending to return after the Sabbath to perfume his body and to minister to his corpse. Luke's Gospel exhorts his disciples to pick up their cross at their Baptisms, at the moment of their being offered in sacrifice to God. At Baptism we are told: 'You live now, no longer for yourself alone, but hidden with Christ in God.' We take up our position at the foot of the cross at Baptism. It is the mark of belonging to the family of Jesus. Originally these lines were spoken to the newly baptised person, while they were on their knees as they were signed with the cross – indicating that this is where we, in spirit, are found throughout our entire life.

But the story isn't finished. There is another who appears to meet the child and his parents at the Temple.

> There was also a prophetess named Anna, daughter of Phanuel, of the tribe of Asher. After leaving her father's home, she had been seven years with her husband, and since then she had been continually about the Temple serving God as a widow night and day in fasting and prayer. She was now eighty-four. Coming up at that time, she gave praise to God and spoke of the child to all who looked forward to the deliverance of Jerusalem. (Lk 2:36-38)

Here is an old woman, a widow who serves God in the Temple, a prophet, one who calls attention to injustice and announces that there will be judgement. There will be restitution and justice. There is hope for those who wait and believe and endure. She praises God and becomes the first preacher, the one who publicly witnesses to who and what this child is to all who will listen and take it to heart. She speaks of the child to all who look forward to the deliverance of Jerusalem. She speaks of liberation, of freedom from captivity, of being drawn out of the darkness of the dungeon into the bright, searing light of truth as the people of God. She has fasted and prayed all her life, and this fasting of the heart has given her the eyes of faith so she can reveal the presence of God in their midst and preach the good news. Her heart and the secret thoughts of her soul are revealed. This is the moment of her revelation.

Again we know little about her. She is a figure of mystery and stands for many in the tradition and in our lives. The tribe to which she belongs, Asher, is one of the ten 'lost' tribes. Any trace of these tribes were lost after the fall of the Northern Kingdom when they were deported to Assyria in the eighth century BC. And yet here Anna stands, hundreds of years later. Jewish tradition says that she is a 'daughter of Asher' – part of the house of Jacob that went into Egypt. Four hundred years later she was one of those who left in the Exodus (Gn 46:17 and Num 26:46). She is remembered as a unique survivor of the generation of the Fathers who guarded the secret of how to recognise the one who would come to liberate the people from slavery and lead them to the Promised Land, and now she is a survivor, a prophet in her generation who was the one who would recognise the long promised Messiah. So she, as spokeswoman for her people, is in the temple 'and began to praise God and to speak about the child to all who were looking for the redemption of Jerusalem' (Lk 2:38). These two ancient and wise ones, Simeon and Anna, are cherished members of our families too, each family having these faithful ones in our family trees, reminding us and asking us if we are to be a survivor who will carry on the hopes of our people as prophets and prophetesses.

Mary's revelation comes at another time but it begins from the moment she is invited to become the mother of the Messiah. Her response – her way of life – is to treasure all these messages and continually ponder them in her heart. This description of Mary is repeated again and again in Luke's account. It shows how her soul and mind absorbed the Word of God and the will of God as it was revealed daily in her life and history. She learns as she goes along. She said yes and took it from that point imaginatively and creatively in light of the prophecies and dreams of her people, Israel. Her faith in many ways is like ours, based on Word and community, shared prayer and worship, life experience and the difficult process of making choices and living by them.

In some ways she is the first (in Luke) to stake her life on the Word. She takes enormous risks to birth her child and, with Joseph, to keep him alive. She probably thinks of her child in terms of Davidic kings, prophets and the texts of the Messiah's care for justice, peace and the nurturing of the poor in the land. She ponders, seeks understanding, reflects and prays over what is happening to her, her child and her husband, Joseph. This pondering includes fear, worry, sensitivity to events and relationships around her, possibilities of response and action. This is the way she lived and the way we Christians should live: pondering all things in our hearts. The Spirit within her stirred and was released in her words and greetings, as with Elizabeth, and dwelled within her daily, long after she bore her child into the world on that cold night in a cave, with Joseph attending as midwife.

Mary is a believer, not a knower. She believes in her child, and through crises and events she seeks meaning and insight, the gifts of wisdom, understanding and knowledge. The book of Wisdom lyrically describes wisdom as a woman whose spirit is holy, unique, intelligent, moving and graceful, 'an aura of the might of God'. She is the one who produces 'friends of God and prophets, and even takes precedence over the light'. The woman Mary is such a spirit, 'a pure effusion of the glory of the Almighty, the refulgence of eternal light, the image of his goodness, the spotless mirror of the power of God' (Wis 6:12-21, 7:22-30). Throughout the early chapters of Luke, Mary is portrayed as 'keeping all these things in her heart' (2:19). She is silent, seeking to understand and know her God and her child and God's will for her daily life. Simple, ordinary human occurrences are her path to knowledge. She experiences conversion, insight and ever-deepening awareness and love of God by the way God deals with her, in her present reality.

She is married to Joseph, who in his way was also the 'first' to stake his life on the Word (in Matthew) and the will of the Lord that he heard in his dream of the angel quoting scripture. This angel told him to have no fear and to take Mary into his home as his wife and to be the father of this child by naming him. He lives and experiences God in the same ways. Boff describes it as follows:

> The sense of Joseph's discourse is the following: he feels involved in an event that mysteriously has to do with God. He embraces, with surprise and anguish, his involvement (cf. Mt 1:19), perhaps without understanding its full implications. But as he is a man that leads his life in the light of God (as any other just man in Israel [cf. Mt 1:19]) and because he has a lot of faith in the intent of the Mystery, he kept all these things in his heart, just as Mary (cf. Luke 2:51).
>
> This completely un-ambitious and upright attitude of entrusting the Unknown-known is enough to confirm his active participation and his substantial cooperation in the mystery of the Spirit overshadowing Mary and of the Word dwelling in Jesus. Joseph is thus connected with God's self-communication to the world, in the form of personalisation in Mary and of incarnation in Jesus ... He is presented as the shadow of the Father ... [3]

Joseph and Mary are husband and wife. Chapter 4 of *Amoris Laetitia*, 'Love in Marriage', speaks of love in the sacrament of marriage. It is descriptive of Joseph and Mary's marriage as well as of others.

> After the love that unites us to God, conjugal love is the 'greatest form of friendship.' It is a union possessing all the traits of a good friendship: concern for the good of the other, reciprocity, intimacy, warmth, stability and the resemblance born of a shared life. Marriage joins to all this an indissoluble exclusivity expressed in the stable commitment to share and shape together the whole of life. [4]

Joseph and Mary are friends! They would have shared and reflected together from the beginning, bound in love, by grace and the Spirit. They reflect strongly these words that describe 'Marriage [as] the icon

---

3 Boff, *Saint Joseph*, op. cit., pp. 103–4.

4 AL, 123, quoting Thomas Aquinas, *Summa Contra Gentiles III*; cf. Aristotle, *Nicomachean Ethics*, 8, 12 (ed. Bywater, Oxford, 1984), 174.

of God's love for us. Indeed, God is also communion: the three Persons of the Father, the Son and Spirit live eternally in perfect unity. And this is precisely the mystery of marriage: God makes of the two spouses one single existence.'[5]

This passionate relationship is described in the Song of Songs, 'the Bible's paean to human love'.[6] Joseph, who is righteous and just, and Mary, who sings the wonders God has done for his people, are a couple that grow into being husband and wife, friends and the parents of Jesus in the same way that other couples do as they commit themselves to one another and seek to create a future together for their children. Joseph and Mary provided models of devoted Jewish parents teaching the Law and the Prophets by their own lives.

What Joseph and Mary learned in their musings and prayer and silent work, they passed on to their child. We are told that he grew 'in stature and strength and was filled with wisdom: the grace of God was upon him' (Lk 2:40). Jesus was taught, nourished and formed by this man and woman who knew God and sought to love him with all their heart and soul and mind and strength in obedience to the command of the Torah. Joseph is Jesus' father, teacher and first concrete image of the love of God, whom he will call Father. Mary is Jesus' mother who shares her overshadowing of the Spirit of God with him. It is from their stories of what they have known of God that Jesus will distill and refine the good news that God loves us, even when we are unaware of that love or our need for it. All their lives they will ponder, wonder and pray over how God deals with them; how God saves them and the world through the freedom and the acceptance of being Jesus' father and mother in all his formative years. They are friends with one another, friends with God, and servants and parents who will in time become disciples of their child.

This stance of 'pondering and treasuring all these things in their hearts', this way of living, will be their shared way of life. The long process of analysis and critical understanding of truth has begun and will not end.

---

5 Ibid., 121, quoting *Catechesis* (2 April 2014): *L'Osservatore Romano* (3 April 2014), p. 8.

6 Don Vernet's two volumes on Joseph and Mary inscribe their love in this biblical frame. His Mary contemplates the Song of Songs as her vocation to love only God, but she realises that this love can be lived out in the framework of a marriage with Joseph. See *Tu Giuseppe*, 31, 'A Holy Family? A Biblical Meditation on Jesus' family in the Synoptic Gospels' in David M. Neuhaus SJ, op. cit., p. 34.

Reflection, contemplation upon events and relationships, analysis – these are the constant and systematic channels of insight and growth into adult faith for these first disciples and for all of us. They extend and deepen their awareness, and ours, of the world and the role each play in the kingdom of God.

All of this is intimated in the encounters in the temple with Simeon and Anna when they meet and recognise who this child is. The revelation they have waited for in faithfulness for so long is now realised and they both praise God. Perhaps Mary's own moment of revelation does not come until much later, as it is recorded in John's Gospel at the end of Jesus' life. Mary is then middle-aged and has watched her child grow into a teacher, a rabbi, a prophet and the sign of contradiction. She has seen the darkness rise against him, seeking to block out the light. He is dying by crucifixion, being slaughtered legally though unjustly, and she is witness, standing at the foot of the cross.

> Near the cross of Jesus stood his mother, his mother's sister Mary, who was the wife of Cleophas, and Mary of Magdala. When Jesus saw the Mother, and the disciple, he said to the Mother, 'Woman, this is your son.' Then he said to the disciple, 'There is your mother.' And from that moment the disciple took her to his own home. (Jn 19:25-27)

This passage is about the cross and about family. Jesus is giving Mary to the disciple, to all disciples, to the Church, to his family. She is not just his mother but mother to all. In death, Jesus separates himself from his mother, as mother. She is mother now because she has learned to mother the disciples, the Church, and all those in need, those who suffer and die unjustly. She has learned to be as God, as mother hen, as her child has been. Anything she has felt or experienced or known of him, Jesus, the saviour, she must now share with his disciples.

Joseph had cared for a child not his own and a woman he befriended to save them from shame and violent death. Jesus took care of his mother, a widow. In this family, blood ties are not the basis of intimacy and closeness: need and faithful love make us parent and child. When Mary is left with no child of her own, she is given God's family. All those left with nothing are given to us, and we are to take them into our homes. Mary is first disciple and follower. The blood that binds is not the blood she birthed him in but the blood of the cross that birthed her into his family.

This sign of contradiction, this sword separates Jesus and his mother and places her in a new relationship to all those who are the children of God. This is done for our benefit and for hers as well. The family of God is created in word, obedience, witness and suffering. We are called to be as close to God as Mary was and closer by being mother, brother and sister to all those who are victims. The sword cuts though all hearts, including Mary's. We are offered intimacy if we let the sword pierce our heart and the Word cut through all our relationships. The cross reveals our hearts and what we are – and what we are not. As a disciple Mary was at the foot of the cross all her life, as all disciples are called to be. And so was Joseph.

Mary's offering is her body, soul and mind along with her child's life. She is a strong, determined woman who spends much of her life hidden in the recesses of small towns, in exile and solitude. Her soul is darkened by secrecy and sorrow, a woman separated from all others in blessing and pain. She is our model for dealing with desolation, anguish and austerity in a world where ordinary people are too often caught in terror and injustice.

Mary must live with and absorb the inhuman dimensions of evil and dare to touch events such as slaughter, rejection, exile, brutality, lies and death. She lives with wrenching truths many of us avoid, but the horror of life demands outrage, witness against and a simplicity that defends life and humanity. She must wrench spiritual insight and courage from the cross; doing so is fundamental to her belief and holiness. Jesus bears his cross, and she bears her child, the Word of God, and her own cross. Indeed, intimacy or closeness with God involves shared pain and sorrow as well as rejoicing in the Lord. This woman has no life of her own. She handed it over to God.

Mary is both a woman of blessings and a woman of woes. In the beginning of the Gospels the blessings abound. There are Beatitudes, from the angel Gabriel and from Elizabeth, and they are powerful: 'Hail, full of grace, the Lord is with you … You have found favour with God.' Mary is a blessing, a beatitude, not so much because of what she does but because of who she is, one of the lowly on whom God looks with special tenderness and mercy. When she sings, it is to celebrate and proclaim the marvels of this God, who has accomplished such deeds of forgiveness and restoration and continues to perform miracles through her out of unfathomable love. In her lowliness and poverty, Mary is aware of her total dependence on God. All her hope is in the promises God has made to the people.

Mary's blessings are our blessings. We are the highly favoured sons and daughters of God from our Baptism. We are the ones who believe the promises God makes to those who live on the divine Word. We learn from Mary how to be a blessing for others.

In the Gospels, Mary is the portrait of those to whom the promises of Yahweh are given and through whom they are fulfilled. It is through Mary and Joseph that the reign of mercy, the reign of peace with justice, enters the world to stay. Christ is himself the fleshing out of that reign no less in the womb than in the crib or on the cross. It is Mary who labours first that Christ might be born, then stands by him as he dies, mother to all beloved disciples at the birth of the Church. Mary is the one who mourns as well as rejoices; she weeps for her son as well as sings for him. At the foot of the cross, Mary is seen in her most terrible sorrow as one of the blessed in the kingdom. This is where we all stand, at the foot of the cross as followers and friends of Jesus. We are to be this poor in spirit, mourning, hungering and thirsting for justice, suffering for righteousness and peace. We are to be merciful, forgiving in our hearts for those who murder our brothers and sisters. At the foot of the cross we are to stand with Mary and the other disciples, as the disciple that Jesus loved, and gather within us all the anguish and misery of those who suffer with others, of all who stand with the outcast, and of all who are deserted by everyone they ever counted on.

Christ in his passion embodies the Beatitudes lived to their ultimate consequences. His mother, in her compassion at the cross, images the same reality in a different way. Mary stands for all who choose freely to take upon themselves the suffering of those cursed in the eyes of the world and blessed in the eyes of God. She suffers in her own heart the wounds inflicted upon her child. In bearing this pain, she bears the suffering of all who take up their cross. At the cross she becomes mother of all Christ's disciples, and they learn from her, just as he did, the meaning of poverty, humility, obedience and mercy. She is the Mother of the Church and all who choose to be one with the wounded of the world.

One facet of this mother love is found in a Native American story about the first butterflies. This version closely resembles one by Wahwahskgone.

Once upon a time, long ago, human twins were born to Spirit Woman. She nurtured them, but often had birds and animals help her care for them. All the animals played with them and gave them food and skins and furs to ease their days and nights, and they were always protected by the dogs and wolves. The water creatures – muskrat, beaver, and otter – bathed them and taught them how to swim. All the animals and birds thought of the children as their own, along with their small ones.

But after a while the animals noticed that the children weren't growing like the other baby animals and birds. They were healthy, because they were fed doe's milk and meat from the animals' catches, and they were happy because they loved to splash and play with otter's children. But the animals were concerned and watched the children closely. They were not growing as they should. Finally, they went to Nanabush and told him of the problem. He agreed that the children were not growing. He gathered all the animals together and said, 'You have cared for the children well, in fact, too well. They have everything they need. In fact, they have more than what they need. They have everything given to them, even before they know they want it, and so they don't need to get up and walk on their own two feet. I will think about this and come up with a way to teach them how to walk.'

Nanabush went off into the forest and prayed to the Great Spirit. He climbed into the mountains and prayed to the one who is protector of the children and asked what he should do to help the young ones learn to walk on their own. And the Great Spirit answered his prayer. He was told to go down the mountain to the quick running streams of cold, clear water and to look for stones, thousands of tiny, sparking pebbles. He obeyed and found the stones and collected hundreds of them: blue and silver, white and pink, yellow and black stones. Soon he had a huge pile of them. Then he sat with the stones and watched them. They didn't do anything. They were just stones. He grew bored and restless and took one of them and tossed it into the air. Then he skimmed another across the face of the waters. Again and again he threw them into the air and caught them again. Then, on the another throw, nothing returned to his hand! Nanabush looked up and saw a tiny sparkling winged creature. Quickly he threw all up into the air, thousands of them, and watched in fascination as they changed into tiny, flying, bright things. They fluttered about and landed in his hair and on his arms. Soon he was covered with the tiny things, swaddled in clouds of them. They were butterflies.

Nanabush went back to the animals and to the young children, the twins, with his new creatures. The children laughed and waved their arms and hands and yelled and screamed and played with the butterflies. Soon they stretched their legs and stood up and ran, waving their arms like butterflies and trying to catch them with their hands. The children learned to walk, run and jump. And butterflies to this day fly before and all around us to make us stretch and reach beyond where we are.[7]

Mary is somehow God's first butterfly, given to us to make us stretch beyond our limited understandings of mother, love, family, relationship and intimacy. God lured her with blessings and the Word, and God lures us with those same blessings and the Word and the gift of his mother. The gifts are passed along. Relationships are not for clinging or even for security but for reaching and running after and seeking beyond our current boundaries. Our lives are to sparkle and dance and lure others into the arms of God. Mary's life is a dance to imitate, but the steps are ours to learn, and no dance is the same. What is important is to grow up, walk on our own two feet, and run after the Spirit's gifts. A mother's love stretches us and makes us imitate the love we have been given so graciously.

IN THE SHADOW OF THE FATHER'S HOUSE
The daily life of Jesus, Mary and Joseph is marked by ritual, worship and the seasons of the liturgy of the Jewish people. Every year the family went to Jerusalem for the Feast of the Passover, as was customary (Lk 2:41).

---

7   Ojibway legend. One version may be found in Basil H. Johnson, *Tales the Elders Told* (Canada: Royal Ontario Museum, 1981).

First and foremost, this family obeys the laws and customs that hold the people together. Primary to this bonding is the Feast of the Passover, the feast of liberation and commemoration of the power and mercy of God in hearing the cry of the slaves in Egypt. This feast is the making of a people, a holy people of priests, prophets and kings who belong to the Lord and reveal to the nations God's presence with them in justice, peace and the promise of everlasting freedom and rest.

When Jesus is twelve, ready to become an adult believer, they go again to the holy city Jerusalem, but this time, unbeknownst to his parents, Jesus remains behind, when the time of worship and Jesus' bar mitzvah is completed. He is now a mature Jewish man, subject to all the responsibilities and practices of a believer.

When Mary and Joseph realise he is not travelling with their relatives or friends, they retrace their steps. After searching for him for three days, they find him in the Temple 'sitting among the teachers, listening to them and asking questions. And all the people were amazed at his understanding and his answers.'

Jesus has come of age. He is studying and delving into his tradition, the practice and prayers and history of his people's ways with God. He already knows his own mind and soul and is learning who he is as a child of Israel, a child of God called to be prophet, teacher and believer. He is going beyond his parents in understanding, belief and knowledge, under the guidance of the Spirit.

Jesus joins with others in the Temple galleries, pilgrims and students of the law and scriptures. He learns and questions and probes on his own. He is breaking with childhood and his previous relationship with family, relatives, friends and neighbours. Now he is an adult, responsible for his own choices and actions. His first break is with his parents, specifically his mother. It is she who questions him and rebukes him:

'Son, why have you done this to us? Don't you realise that your father and I have been full of sorrow while searching for you?' Then he said to them, 'Why were you looking for me? Did you not know that I must be in my Father's house?' But they did not understand this answer.

Jesus went down with them, returning to Nazareth, and he continued to be under their authority. As for his mother, she kept all

these things in her heart. And Jesus increased in wisdom and age and
in divine and human grace. (Lk 2:48-52)

Jesus is no longer a child who learns primarily from his parents and family.
Now he learns from the Spirit, history, and in his own right. And Mary
and Joseph will learn from him as he grows in wisdom and grace before
God and the community in Nazareth. He is still under their authority
and obeys them, but the quality of his obedience has shifted to an inner
authority and understanding born of commitment to the will of God.
Though he stays with his parents, he has broken ties with them religiously,
emotionally and psychologically. He is becoming conscious of being
the beloved Son of God. He is realising that anywhere the scriptures are
loved, cherished, studied and put into practice is his Father's house, not
just the Temple.

Mary and Joseph are described as full of sorrow while searching for
him, but he doesn't seem to appreciate their concern. Should they not
know where he is? He is now an adult, ritually and in spirit and practice.
They must get used to him living his own life and going his own way, the
way of the Father. There are no ties on earth that are more important than
the tie to God the Father and the kingdom coming on earth in the Word
of God. Joseph and Mary must learn to give Jesus growing room. He is
their obedient son by choice, out of reverence and respect for them as
his parents. But now he follows Another.

In Luke's Gospel the first misunderstanding Jesus has with another
person is with his mother. Mary does not understand, and so she returns
to reflection, thought and prayer, seeking to learn from the Spirit what her
growing son is about: who he is and what he is becoming. From now on,
Mary is the one who must learn and grow in belief. Her son is Messiah,
Lord, rabbi, prophet, and more. She does not know him. Her mind and
heart must be stretched and opened to become a disciple, just as every
other person who meets him must choose and change.

We do not meet Mary again in Luke until after the Resurrection, in
the Acts of the Apostles (which is really a continuation of Luke's Gospel).
After the Ascension all the remaining disciples have returned to Jerusalem
where they are waiting for the coming of the Paraclete, the Advocate, the
promised presence of the Lord in his Spirit. The disciples are all listed

by name and then there is mention of others: 'All of these together gave themselves to constant prayer. With them were some women and also Mary, the mother of Jesus, and his brothers' (Acts 1:14). We are back to the specific reference to Jesus' true family – his disciples and those who are followers with them; some women and Mary, his mother and brothers, his blood relatives. His blood relatives are members of his new community only by reason of prayer and the coming of the Spirit. Luke's last mention of Mary is as a member of the early Christian community, one of those who received the Spirit at Pentecost. When the Spirit comes upon the Church, Mary disappears into its midst, in silence, into the life described in Acts:

> They were faithful to the teaching of the apostles, the common life of sharing, the breaking of the bread and the prayers. A holy fear came upon all the people, for many wonders and miraculous signs were done by the apostles. Now all the believers lived together and shared all their belongings. They would sell their property and all they had and distribute the proceeds to others according to their need. Each day they met together in the Temple area; they broke bread in their homes; they shared their food with great joy and simplicity of heart; they praised God and won the peoples' favour. And every day the Lord added to their number those who were being saved. (Acts 2:42-47)

Mary is now one of many believers, first in Jerusalem and then, according to tradition, in Ephesus, living with Mary of Magdala and John, who took her into his home. The ancient belief is that Mary lives there, sharing food and breaking bread, praying and rejoicing until she dies at the age of ninety-two. She lives as disciple and follower of Jesus in the Church, growing, as once she watched her child grow, in wisdom, age and grace before God and the community. She treasures all these things in her heart, watching the Spirit work in the Church and in the world and in the lives and hearts of those around her, as the good news is preached and the Word is brought into the world far beyond her doorstep.

She grows old, singular and apart, alone with her memories, her soul, and his friends, whose lives have been altered radically, as hers was, by their association with Jesus the Christ, the Son of God.

There are stories in the Gospel, stories Jesus told, that have echoes of what he learned from her, what she meant to him. In Luke's and Mark's Gospels, Jesus tells his disciples to look at a widow. He points her out to them, telling them that she is the image of discipleship, hidden and unknown except for his eyes.

Jesus sees rich people putting their gifts into the treasure box; he also sees a poor widow dropping in two small coins. And he says, 'Truly, I tell you, this poor widow put in more than all of them. For all gave an offering from their plenty, but she instead, out of her poverty, gave everything she had to live on' (Lk 21:1-4).

She, out of her poverty, gave all she had – she gave her child, her privileged relationship as mother to him, her years of service and anonymity and ordinariness, her simplicity and obedience to the Word. Nothing spectacular, nothing extraordinary, just faithfulness, constant conversion and growth in grace, enduring daily and forgiving, reconciling and healing, restoring arid living with mercy and tender regard for all the believers. She forgave Peter his betrayal, Judas his treachery and loss of faith, all the disciples who ran in fear and cowardice, and all the people he had healed and helped and drawn back into the community's embrace, who turned from him in times of crisis and danger. She forgave all the pettiness and lived patiently with all the misunderstandings of the fledgling Church and its dissenting groups and leaders.

This community included many of the widowed, those single for the kingdom, and repentant sinners, beloved of the Master and seen as disciples, a group privately obedient and attentive to the community's needs of body and soul. These were servants to the servants, servants to those more public members who suffered and preached and died violently, witnesses to the cross as the seed of the Church's growth over long decades of endurance and growth in belief. These too were mother, brother and sister to Jesus' Spirit in the world. Their faith, their prayer and contemplation, their long, loving look at reality – especially reality that is hard to look at and understand even with the grace of the Spirit – give sustenance and depth of insight to believers. The power of the Spirit resides within the heart of the community. Mary is a model disciple, one who believed the words that the Lord had promised to her and then went on to believe more and more and more until resurrection overshadowed all belief and birthed a hope that demanded pure faith. Her child is the Son of God, and she is invited into relationship as daughter to God.

The Church celebrates Mary's fiat, her surrender to God, on 25 March, the Feast of the Annunciation or Feast of the Incarnation. God extended the invitation to intimacy and Mary said yes, simply and obediently. We are invited to do as she did. On 25 March 1980, Archbishop Oscar Romero was killed while he said Mass in the bombed cathedral in San Salvador. And so, on the same day we celebrate the martyrdom of a disciple and the announcement of the power of grace over hate. The two events are the two sides of blessing. In one of his sermons, Romero said:

> They simply want to live! When I talk to a *campesino* whose family is so poor that his children are dying from hunger, it is not acceptable for him to say, 'It is the will of God'. It is not the will of God! It is not the will of God for people to suffer. It is the will of man. It is the poor who make us comprehend the reality around us. They mirror the suffering Christ, they are Christ! ... If you are going to work with the poor, then be ready to suffer their destiny. This may mean that you too may disappear, be captured, tortured, and be found dead.

Oscar Romero is dead, but his presence is still felt. He has now been beatified. When his people gather together to celebrate liturgy, they call out a litany of those who have suffered and died with the people and the people answer: '*Presente*.' And in every place where there is a struggle for justice and human dignity, Mary, who was poor and oppressed, is called upon in a litany of honour and respect. And the people all answer: '*Presente*, Maria!' Whenever her presence is needed, Mary's name is spoken. She disappears in the scriptures into the heart of the Church and reappears in the life and affections of the followers of the Word.

JOSEPH: SHADOW OF THE FATHER

But what of Joseph? Joseph and Mary return together to Nazareth having turned a corner in their relationship with their child Jesus who is becoming a person in his own right – what he was born to be and came into this world to be – Jesus, the one who saves us and liberates us to become the beloved children of God; Immanuel, our God with us in flesh, body and soul; Son of Man, friend of the poor and the beloved Son of God.

Joseph and Mary are married, committed to their own relationship with ever deeper faithfulness, as man and woman, as husband and wife, as Jews living in their extended family and with their people who live in occupied territory under the harsh heel of the Roman forces. Their lives are ordinary and yet filled with passionate devotion to God, obedience to the daily and seasonal rituals of their religion and to their own mutual love and friendship.

Their love is all-encompassing. In the Apostolic Exhortation of Pope Francis we read: 'such a love, bringing together the human and the divine, leads the partners to a free and mutual self-giving, experienced in tenderness and action, and permeating their entire lives.'[8]

It continues with seeking to describe the joy that such a relationship can foster, quoting Thomas Aquinas: 'the word "joy" refers to an expansion of the heart.'[9] This is followed by the reminder that:

> Marital joy can be experienced even amid sorrow; it involves accepting that marriage is an inevitable mixture of enjoyment and struggles, tensions and repose, pain and relief, satisfactions and longings, annoyances and pleasures, but always on the path of friendship, which inspires married couples to care for one another.[10]

They help and serve each other.

The Holy Spirit overshadowed Mary, and from the seeding of the Word within her, stayed and dwelled in her. In prayers Mary is sometimes referred to as the 'Ark of the Covenant', seeking to describe how the Spirit resided in her as a permanent presence, mysteriously growing more mature and strong with her. This is the presence we are given, as 'the first gift given to those who believe' at our Baptism and Confirmation.

What we often ignore or seem to be unconscious of is that this also was the experience of Joseph, the believer who said yes to God as deeply as she did. This is the way it is described theologically:

---

8   AL, 125, quoting *Gaudium et Spes*, 49.
9   Ibid., 126, referencing *Summa Theologiae* I–II, q, art. 3, ad 3.
10 Ibid.

Within this framework, to say that Saint Joseph is the shadow of the Father means to recognise that the Father inhabits him and that the Father is permanently and consistently present in him. I would say that the Father is personalised in Saint Joseph. But this presence of the Father is not directly announced; rather it is hidden in Joseph. What we see is the father Joseph, but what is hidden in him is the celestial Father. This reasoning enriches our understanding of the Holy Trinity's self-communication to the world. It is not the case that only the Son and the Holy Spirit came amongst us: the Father also came amongst us.[11]

The presence or the shadow of the Father is more hidden, more silent in Joseph, but just as revelatory. Joseph's relationship with Mary, with Jesus and in his extended family and community speaks of the characteristics of fathering another person. Leonardo Boff lists as follows the virtues and expressions that we know from the scriptures about how Joseph lives. He shows 'the determination to make a decision when faced with a complex problem' (like the situation with Mary's pregnancy). He has a 'strong sense of duty' even when it entails the census in Bethlehem, and he is midwife to Mary as she labours to give birth. And as a Jew he fulfils his obligations as regards the temple, to worship, and the rituals of daily Jewish life – taking Jesus to Jerusalem as is the custom for the boy's coming of age as a Jew. He is courageous by 'facing up to the risk of persecution by Herod, by facing up to the anguish and austerity of a hasty escape into exile in Egypt' and deciding when it is safe to return and where to settle so that they might be a family, living in relative peace in occupied territory. 'As a father, he exercised authority and imposed limits' – we know this because we are told that after his experience in the temple, Jesus returned and 'was obedient to them' (Lk 2:51)

Joseph then was a bridge between the family and society. Jesus is known and accepted as the son of Joseph in Jewish society, and Joseph passes onto him his craft, his trade of carpentry. We know this from expressions found in the Gospels (cf. Mt 13:54-56; Lk 4:25; Jn 1:45, 6:42). Perhaps the most telling and important is this last shadow and trace of the Father in Joseph in relation to Jesus.

---

11 Boff, *Saint Joseph*, op. cit., p. 106.

Lastly, the healthy and vigorous paternity of Joseph served as a basis for Jesus' spiritual experience as he calls God *abba*. If Jesus showed extreme intimacy with God in his public life by calling him the infantile term 'Daddy' (*'abba'*), this means that he lived a similar experience of extreme intimacy with his father Joseph.

... Saint Joseph is an exemplary figure whom we can connect with and from whom we can learn important lessons. This is especially the case for fathers in the twenty-first century; who live in a model of civilization that is extremely different and who are in search of a kind of identity that is appropriate for our times.

Saint Joseph helps us rescue fatherhood. His example of fatherhood can enrich a father's identity and provide some impetus while facing the challenges of modern society, especially the challenges of this globalised age of humanity.[12]

Together, Joseph and Mary revealed God to Jesus and taught him how to be a human being, a man, a Jew, and gave him the glimpses and seeds of what he would become as he 'grew in wisdom, age and grace' before them and among all those around him. Their marriage, their friendship, their ways of being parents with him educated him and formed him physically and mentally as their child while the Spirit of God formed and matured him into who he became as a beloved Child of God.

We know little or nothing except what we have gleaned from history and culture about what their daily lives were like, as part of an ordinary family, humbly (living close to the earth) in a backwater village of Nazareth, among those who were the butt of jokes (nothing good comes out of there!), among people unnoticed, anonymous and among the poorest of the poor. They existed in their extended family in the midst of uncertainty, in the constant presence of the Roman army, and devoted themselves to years of faithfulness, waiting with their people for the coming of the one who would set them free and be the presence of justice and peace among them. They were playing an enormous role in who Jesus became but they were only aware of passing on their belief, their traditions and their faith by the way they lived together.

---

12 Ibid., pp. 154–5.

Joseph is a man of mystery and of overpowering silence and unknownness. He says absolutely nothing in any of the Gospels. We know him only by his work, his actions and his relationships with his family. Joseph disappears into this family and then dies sometime before Jesus is baptised and begins to be the prophet, healer, teacher and preacher of the Good News to the poor, leaving Mary as a widow, in the care of the rest of the family. He believes in his son, his child taken into his care and his heart, but what does he know except what the Spirit would teach him in the depths of his soul and spirit. More than any other, besides Joseph being a just man, he is a man of silence. But silence can be filled with understanding and insight that one is not able to put into words, but still seeps through one's person, decisions and actions.

> The greatest things are accomplished in silence – not in the clamour and display of superficial eventfulness, but in the deep clarity of inner vision; in the almost imperceptible start of decision, in quiet overcoming and hidden sacrifice. Spiritual conception happens when the heart is quickened by love, and the free will stirs to action. The silent forces are the strong forces.[13]

Perhaps one can learn most about Joseph as a father and as a shadow of God our Father by praying as a father for our own children and those we help to grow up to be the beloved children of God, sharing our lives and faith with them. It does not matter if one is a man or a woman, these traits of the Father are now buried deep in all of us who call God, Our Father. But there is a prayer to Saint Joseph that is found in Leonardo Boff's book that can open us to ways of praying and living that echo Joseph and Jesus who is 'like father, like son'.

---

13 Romano Guardini, *The Lord*, trans. Elinor Castendyk Briefs (Washington, DC: Gateway, 1954; 1982), p. 15.

Prayer to Joseph

Dear Saint Joseph,

You were a worker as we are and you know tiredness and sweat. Help us guarantee work for all.

You were a just man who conducted, in your workplace and in the community a life of integrity at the service of God and others. Make us also good in our works and aware of the needs of others.

You were the husband who took Mary already pregnant by the Holy Spirit into your home. Make our parents welcome the lives that God sends them.

You accepted to be the father of Jesus and you took care of him against those who wanted to kill him, and you protected him during your escape into Egypt. Make our parents protect their sons and daughters against addictive drugs and against serious illnesses.

You were Jesus' educator, teaching him to read the scriptures and introducing him to the traditions of your people. Make us continue our family piety and always remember God in everything we do.

* * *

Dear Saint Joseph,

In your human face we see portrayed the face of the divine Father. May He welcome us, protect us, and provide us with the assurance that we walk in the palm of His hand.

Show us, Saint Joseph, the power of your fatherhood. Give us determination in the face of problems, courage in the face of peril, awareness of the limits of our powers, and infinite trust in the celestial Father.

We ask all of these in the power of the Father, in the love of the Son, and in the zeal of the Holy Spirit. Amen.[14]

---

14 Boff, *Saint Joseph*, op. cit., pp. 162–3.

Chapter 7
Making Disciples by Becoming Disciples: The Children

MARY AS THE CATECHUMEN (LUKE 1 AND 2)

There is an old Jewish story told of a rabbi of Berditchev and a student who went to visit him, to study with him, learn from him, question him about a portion of the Torah. He entered the rabbi's room and was surprised to see the man pacing up and down, not in thought, but in ecstatic musings on the scripture. He stood there, a bit embarrassed, until the rabbi suddenly looked up, saw him, as though he recognised him, and said, 'Perhaps it is all true after all!' The student was confused and didn't know what to say. He had studied and was pretty sure he knew what the texts meant – he just had some questions about details, specific meanings of words and how the text might be linked to other scripture passages.

He just stood there and wondered what the rabbi was trying to tell him. Again the rabbi turned to him and said: 'You have feasted on the scriptures and think you know that piece, that you understand its meaning. What do you know? Remember that our sages told us that there are at least forty-seven meanings to every passage, every phrase and letter, even to every piece of punctuation and accent! What if there is another interpretation of the passage? What if we are stuck in the traditional one? What if it is all true! What if we are just beginning to understand? What if?'

And those words of the rabbi, the scripture scholar, beat on his heart and echoed in his mind and roared in his ears, and he went back to the text. This time he questioned whether he was resisting deeper meanings. This time he wondered what it was saying about him, not about the prophets and great looming figures of his ancestors. This time he stood in awe of the text and heard it as written for him, intent on shattering his usual ways of perceiving reality and applying the Torah to his life.

And that became the refrain of his life: What if? What if it is all true? What if we don't know anything? What if we are resisting what the Holy One, blessed be his Name, is saying to us now? What if?

This story is perfect to open this chapter on an alternative reading, a fresh and perhaps bold reading, of the first two chapters of Luke's Gospel that we traditionally read as only about Jesus born of Mary betrothed to Joseph. What if it's about us as much as it is about Mary? What if it's about the formation of believers? What if it's about all those beginning to believe in the Gospel, a primer for those we call catechumens going through the Rite of Christian Initiation of Adults, preparing for Baptism, Confirmation and Eucharist? What if Mary is the icon of every new believer in Luke's primarily Gentile community who fulfils the texts of the synoptic Gospels of a true disciple being one 'who hears the word of God and puts it into practice'? What if we are to respond not only with Mary but as Mary in these chapters? What if what happens to Mary happens to us just as truly, just as deeply – not biologically but as religiously, which is more powerful? Let us try to read this text of the scripture without resistance, relying on some of the older interpretations but applying them more intimately to each of us 'highly favoured daughters and sons of God'.

But even more importantly, what if this reading of the first two chapters of Luke that forms the basis of 'making new Christians' is the best way to pass on our faith, our belief and the practice of our religion to our children – one of the primary duties of all parents within their families along with drawing them more deeply into the life of the Church. The Exhortation in Chapter 5 of *Amoris Laetitia*, 'Love Made Fruitful', which looks at children in our families in the world, begins with this beautiful reminder on the blessing and the gift of any child.

> The gift of a new child, entrusted by the Lord to a father and mother, begins with acceptance, continues with lifelong protection and has as its final goal the joy of eternal life. By serenely contemplating the ultimate fulfilment of each human person, parents will be even more aware of the precious gift entrusted to them. For God allows parents to choose the name by which he himself will call their child for all eternity.[1]

---

1   AL, 166, referencing *Gaudium et Spes*, 51: 'Let us all be convinced that human life and its transmission are realities whose meaning is not limited by the horizons of this life only: their true evaluation and full meaning can only be understood in reference to our eternal destiny.'

If this is true, then perhaps one of the best ways to teach our children is to experience being a catechumen ourselves as adults and then draw our children into the process and have them experience the rite with us at specific ages and liturgical times over the process of their growing in wisdom and age and grace. This is as Jesus did when he learned from his parents Joseph and Mary how to become a faithful Jewish child and mature adult within the extended family, the synagogue and society into which he was born. Most adult Catholics/Christians have not known this ancient experience of what it means to be made a Christian within the community. But having this Rite serve as the foundation of all education and practice for our children would be a way for them to grow into the Body of Christ and the community of Church, both in their families and parishes, preparing them for being a member of God's Community of Beloved Disciples across the world.

Reading this chapter and thinking about it in terms of continuing education for adults, even those already baptised and then seeking to apply it to all members of our families in parishes and dioceses can serve as a pastoral experience to deepen everyone's faith. Even to have a version of it as preparation for any of the sacraments, including marriage, could lay the foundation for the kingdom in our midst today. The Exhortation speaks of this in Chapter 3 of *Amoris Laetitia*, 'Looking to Jesus: The Vocation of the Family', when it writes of faith:

> Here too I will mention what the Synod Fathers had to say about the light offered by our faith. They began with the gaze of Jesus and spoke of how he 'looked upon the women and men whom he met with love and tenderness, accompanying their steps in truth, patience and mercy as he proclaimed the demands of the Kingdom of God'.[2]

---

2 Ibid., 60, quoting *Relatio Synodi*, 12.

WHO IS MY MOTHER?

A soul that has believed has both conceived and bears
the Word of God and declares God's works.
Let the spirit of Mary be in each of you, so that it rejoices in God.
Bede the Venerable

How do we become followers and friends of Jesus? How do we 'grow in wisdom, age and grace before God and others'? How do children grow into adult, mature disciples of Jesus? How do we become the brothers and sisters of Jesus, beloved of the Father, in the power of the Spirit? In Chapter 5, 'Love Made Fruitful', we are reminded of the basics.

> The family is the setting in which a new life is not only born but also welcomed as a gift of God. Each new life 'allows us to appreciate the utterly gratuitous dimension of love, which never ceases to amaze us. It is the beauty of being loved first: children are loved even before they arrive.' Here we see a reflection of the primacy of God's love, who always takes the initiative, for children 'are loved before having done anything to deserve it.[3]

Never in the body of the first three Gospels is Mary singled out or named. In fact she is seen as part of the family of Joseph and not as a disciple of Jesus. What if the original beginning of Luke's Gospel is Chapter 3, the preaching of John the Baptist and the Baptism of Jesus, with Luke adding the first two chapters afterwards to coincide with the beginning of the Acts of the Apostles? The only time Mary appears in Acts is in the description of the first community in Jerusalem, in the upper room, listing the disciples and believers after the Resurrection. The community is described: 'All these devoted themselves with one accord to prayer, together with some women, and Mary, the mother of Jesus, and his brothers' (Acts 1:12-14).

Then the references to Mary form a 'sandwich', where Mary is used to present the process and model of the catechumen: every person in Luke's community as they become a disciple and in the first chapter of Acts as

---

3 Ibid., 166, quoting *Catechesis* (11 February 2015): *L'Osservatore Romano* (12 February 2015), p. 8.

the initiated believer who is now a disciple among the other disciples. In the first sixty or more years after the Resurrection of Jesus, what if Luke took the references of the common tradition and descriptions of what constitutes a true disciple and was inspired to write what we today would call an RCIA process for all the believers of his community, teaching the theology of being baptised, confirmed and receiving Eucharist and then joining the community as a disciple among disciples seeking to 'hear the word of God and obey it'.

This would make the first two chapters of Luke's Gospel not only or even primarily a historical narrative about the actual birth of Jesus but meant as a theological presentation of what it means to be born as a believer and initiated and confirmed in the Body of Christ, and how to hear the Word of God, the Gospel of Luke, together with others, and to obey it in the community of believers, the Church. Both books, the Gospel and Acts, are directed to Theophilus to instruct and teach him about Jesus, crucified and risen from the dead, and all that Jesus revealed about the Word of God. The word *Theophilus* in Greek means either 'beloved of God' or 'lover of God' and so this name can be everyone who seeks to be more intimate with God in Jesus. There is a statement ascribed to a Theophilus of Antioch which says: 'God is seen by those who are enabled to see God, when they have the eyes of their souls opened'. This Theophilus perhaps is a catechumen, or every catechumen, being drawn into the Church in Luke's community.

And so, in this chapter, we are invited to read the first two chapters of Luke, as not only about Mary and as infancy narratives, but as our story and then as the story of how to catechise our children and initiate them into the lifelong process of becoming disciples of Jesus. What if this is the theological and sacramental experience of every person initiated into a community of believers in Jesus, crucified and risen from the dead, the Word of God made flesh in us, the Body of Christ in the world today? The Gospels are belief statements of a community, written in the inspiration and the power of the Spirit to encourage and remind those who believe of what is necessary for growth in holiness and imitation of Jesus, and for maturing in grace and freedom as a beloved child of God, baptised into the Trinity, obeying the Word of God in a community that is now the Body of Christ on earth, witnessing to the mighty acts of God and God's life-giving love.

The way we first begin to believe is by watching, picking up what is going on in our families and in those around us. Early in the first centuries of the Church, John Chrysostom writes about children in families of those who profess to be believers. 'When we teach our children to be good, to be gentle, to be forgiving, to be generous, to love others, we instil virtue in their souls and reveal the image of God within them. This, then, is our task: to educate both ourselves and our children in godliness; otherwise what answer will we have before Christ's judgement-seat?'

THE ANNOUNCEMENT OF THE BIRTH OF JESUS: THE BAPTISM OF THE BELIEVER

> You are all fellow-travellers.
> God-bearers and temple-bearers, Christ-bearers.
> Ignatius of Antioch

What is difficult and yet crucial to this endeavour of reading the Gospel as about us, rather than historically about Mary and the physical birth of Jesus, is to shift the focus onto oneself, as the one described 'as mother, brother and sister to me', as the one who 'hears the Word of God and obeys it' and to realise and come to believe that everything that is described as happening to Mary is happening, and has actually happened, to us in our Baptism, Confirmation and reception of the Eucharist and the Word of God, the Scripture, into our lives as the source and foundation of our lives as disciples in community.

It begins with the announcement of the mystery of the Incarnation. We already believe that God has become flesh, has become a human being in Jesus, and that now God is to be born in our flesh and we are to accept this good news as fundamentally altering our relationship to God and radically transforming what it means for us to be human, to incarnate God in our flesh and give birth to God in our life as surely as Mary did physically. This is our initiation: our experiencing Baptism, Confirmation and Eucharist in community and what it means for us now, sacramentally, theologically and religiously in our person, in our communities.

This idea is ancient, as reflected in this prayer from the Spanish Mozarabic liturgical rite:

> O Lord, we do not pray that your birth according to the flesh shall
> be renewed as it once occurred. Rather we pray that your invisible
> Godhead may be grafted into us. May that which was then accorded
> in the flesh to Mary alone, now be granted in the Spirit to the Church;
> so that faith unquestioning may conceive you, the Spirit free of all
> corruption may bear you, and the soul overshadowed by the power
> of the Most High may quicken with you ever more. Go not forth from
> us; spring forth rather from within us.

The Word of the Lord comes to us not by an angel (which means
'messenger from God') but in the scriptures, the Gospel, and it comes to
us in our specific circumstances, relationships and geographical locations,
each of us known and named. And the words are addressed to us!

> And coming to her, he said: 'Hail, favoured one! The Lord is with you.'
> But she was greatly troubled at what was said and pondered what sort
> of greeting this might be. Then the angel said to her, 'Do not be afraid,
> for you have found favour with God. Behold, you will conceive in your
> womb and bear a son, and you shall name him Jesus. He will be great
> and will be called Son of the Most High, and the Lord God will give
> him the throne of David his father, and he will rule over the house of
> Jacob forever, and of his kingdom there will be no end.' (Lk 1:28-33)

This is the announcement of the Incarnation, the birth of God in Jesus
into our lives, the coming true of all the promises of the past, the tradition
and waiting of the Jewish people, the presence of the person who is the
hope of the nations, the invitation for each of us to take this Word into
our own minds, hearts, souls and lives and make it the flesh and bone, the
reality of our existence. We, each of us, has found favour with God even
before God is born in us in Baptism, and this good news is meant for every
human being, woman and man, alone, engaged, married, widowed – from
every village and city, for in Jesus the revelation of God, the Incarnation,
happens in daily life, in history, and now is good news of redemption and
salvation for all the people (cf. Lk 1:68). In Jesus we 'have been given
knowledge of salvation through the forgiveness of our sins, because of the
tender mercy of our God by which the daybreak from on high will visit

us to shine on those who sit in darkness and death's shadow, to guide our feet into the path of peace' (Lk 1:77-79, Zechariah's canticle of praise).

For the one ready for Baptism, this greeting of the angel to Mary, and so to the catechumen can be disturbing. The words are troubling (Hail favoured one, the Lord is with you!) and like Mary the catechumen as well as every one of us can wonder what they mean. The word used is *diatataraso*, which means 'perplexing, confusing, and deeply troubling'. And the word for 'wondered' is *dialogizomai*, which means 'trying to figure out why this is happening, trying to come up with reasons for what's happening in her life'. All those preparing for Baptism (and Mary), as well as us in our lives, can find this experience disorienting, throwing them off balance while they try to figure out how to respond. And this is the usual response more often than not to the proclamation of the Gospel. The interruption of God into our lives undoes us and from its conception in our heart and world everything becomes 'what if?'

This proclamation of the Word of God to us is a baptismal confession of what we believe about who Jesus is – the fulfilment of all the earlier Testament's prophecies and God's Word of hope to his people Israel. God is to be 'conceived', seeded in us, and we are summoned to bear the Son of God into the world in our flesh and life, and to stake our lives on Jesus' divinity and humanity as our salvation, our freedom and our life. As members of the community preparing for Baptism and initiation in the Church, we are called to believe in Jesus, crucified and raised from the dead, and become the children of God in the power of the Spirit. And Mary, as every catechumen, asks: how can this be; how will this happen?

> But Mary said to the angel, 'How can this be, since I have no relations with a man?' And the angel said to her in reply, 'The Holy Spirit will come upon you and the power of the Most High will overshadow you. Therefore the child to be born will be called holy, the Son of God.' (Lk 1:34-36)

We must go backwards and forwards, to the presence and coming of the Spirit that accompanies the people of God in the Exodus and to the coming and presence of the Spirit that accompanies and is the presence of God at Pentecost, birthing the community of Church. This is the initiation, the Baptism of one into the Body of Christ. The Holy Spirit comes upon the individual, the power of the Most High overshadows the one baptised – as the cloud overshadowed Jesus and the disciples at the transfiguration (cf. Lk 9:34). It has been said that the Spirit of God needs flesh to act in the world, and at Baptism the Spirit of God seizes the flesh of the baptised person and makes the body of that person God's home, God's temple in the world. God is enfleshed, incarnated in us. At the end of Luke's Gospel in the Easter appearance to his disciples, Jesus says to them: 'Look at my hands and my feet, that it is I myself. Touch me and see, because a ghost does not have flesh and bones as you can see I have' (Lk 24:39-40). We are baptised into the crucified and risen Lord, dying with Christ and rising with Christ to new life.

As Mary will give birth, as a poor uneducated woman of Galilee, in an occupied country, enslaved, and living on hope, so will every one who relies on the Word of God, preached as Good News to the poor, give birth in their flesh. And believing in Jesus as the Son of God, baptised into the Trinity, we become the beloved sons and daughters of God – the brothers, sisters and mothers of Jesus. We each answer, and respond in our baptismal acceptance: 'Behold, I am the handmaid of the Lord. May it be done to me according to your word' (Lk 1:38). And we each say 'Yes', proclaiming our belief in Jesus Christ, Son of God, Saviour, Risen Lord, God incarnate, the Word made flesh in history and now in hope and in our flesh and in the Body of Christ, the Church. Our lives as disciples begin with taking this Word into our ears, our minds and hearts, and beginning the journey of enfleshing the Word in our bodies and lives. We are baptised in the Lord and become the beloved servants of God.

Mary is described as a virgin, which originally meant a young woman of marriageable age. But the word has always had deeper, more theological meanings as well. It means being connected or belonging to no one, but alone before God, filled with grace, and filled with the Spirit. Earlier in the chapter, John the Baptist is described: 'even in his mother's womb he will be filled with the Spirit' (Lk 1:15). It is the Spirit that conceives the Word of God, the seed of holiness and divinity within each of us – Immanuel, God with us. It is the Spirit that seizes our flesh in love, with the same intensity that the Spirit exhibits when tongues of fire come to rest over each member of the community in Acts. In Baptism we are given the same relationship to God the Father, in the power of the Spirit, with Jesus, that Jesus has in the Trinity. We are conceived and born of the Spirit and water.

The Visitation of the Spirit: Confirmation

> Blessed be God, who chose you in Christ!
> Baptismal acclamation of the Roman Rite

And so the newly baptised 'goes in haste' to another and enters the house of Elizabeth who befriends and confirms their promise of belief, their acceptance of the Word of God in their life, and shares knowledge and encouragement with them. We greet others with the Resurrection proclamation: Peace be with you! We have risen to new life and now must learn how to practice resurrection in our lives, but we must learn from others in the community. Listen to the word!

> When Elizabeth heard Mary's greeting, the infant leapt in her womb, and Elizabeth, filled with the Holy Spirit, cried out in a loud voice and said, 'Most blessed are you among women, and blessed is the fruit of your womb. And how does this happen to me, that the mother of my Lord should come to me? For at the moment the sound of your greeting reached my ears, the infant in my womb leapt for joy. Blessed are you who believed that what was spoken to you by the Lord would be fulfilled.' (Lk 1:41-45)

The sound of the Word – the Good News of the Risen Lord – in the world evokes the presence and the power of the Spirit in others. Elizabeth (a godmother, a friend, perhaps even someone you barely know) cries out in a loud voice in recognition. Another Elizabeth (Seton) exhorts us: 'Be attentive to the voice of Grace!' This has always been the sign of the Spirit's presence in prophecy and revelation. And the newly baptised Christian is praised for believing! The seed, the one who goes before the Word, as prophet and as one who prepares the way for repentance that leads to forgiveness, leaps for joy at recognition of the sound of the Good

News now present in the world. Now the Word sounds through us! The Spirit, the third person of the Trinity, lifts and carries the truth in our voices, stirring insight and revelation in others. The word 'person' means literally 'to sound through' (per/sonar). The Spirit sounds through the one baptised who is now confirmed in the power of the Spirit. The fruit of our womb is the Word of God loose in the world in another believer, spreading and connecting with others.

The Magnificat: The Worship and Praise of the Newly Baptised and Confirmed

Thanksgiving belongs to prayer. Thanksgiving is a true inward acknowledgement, we applying ourselves with great reverence and loving fear with all our powers to the work that God moved us to, rejoicing and giving thanks inwardly.
And so the power of the Lord's word enters the soul and enlivens the heart and makes us rejoice in the Lord.
This is the most loving thanksgiving in God's sight.
Julian of Norwich

In response to receiving the Good News, to being baptised, to being confirmed, the Spirit now prays in the mouth and heart and soul of the new Christian, christened and anointed with the Spirit. And all that is sung and proclaimed in glory, in gratitude and in hope, is our prayer, the prayer of another beloved child rejoicing in God our saviour. Let us pray.

My soul proclaims the greatness of the Lord; my spirit rejoices in God my saviour.
For he has looked upon his handmaid's lowliness; behold, from now on all ages call me blessed.
The mighty One has done great things for me, and holy is his name.
His mercy is from age to age on those who fear him.
He has shown might with his arm, dispersed the arrogant of mind and heart.
He has thrown down the rulers from their thrones and lifted up the lowly.

The hungry he has filled with good things; the rich he has sent away empty.

He has helped Israel his servant, remembering his mercy, according to his promise to our ancestors, to Abraham and to his descendants forever. (Lk 1:46-55)

This is the psalm of the new Christian standing in public in the community and sharing their joy, their belief and all that God has done for them, bringing them this far and bringing them into the Church. It is the psalm of the mercy of God, singing through each of us and proclaiming that everything is being radically overturned, in our hearts and in all those who were once arrogant. And all will be made new in the kingdom of God, and God's community of the Body of Christ where the poor are honoured and cared for, and each is given according to their need and the rich go away empty-handed. And the God who hears the cry of the poor makes a people where there are no poor among them. And the psalm continues in hope for a world where the lowly are lifted high, and the violent and those who rule by greed are judged and thrown down. This is the mercy of God in Jesus. This is the presence of God that has been with believers since the beginning and is now doing a new thing, glorious to behold!

Being a virgin (it matters not whether you are male or female, married or single theologically) is connected to being a prophetess. We give birth to the Word of God in the world, and the Spirit comes upon everyone at Pentecost, where the tongues of fire part and come to rest on each, giving them utterance, bold speech and the knowledge of many languages for proclamation on a universal basis. Note that in Isaiah 7:14 is the ancient oft-quoted prophecy of the virgin that 'shall be with child, and bear a son and shall name him Emmanuel.' And in Isaiah 8:3 the prophet 'went to the prophetess and she conceived and bore a son'. We are all prophets now giving birth to the Word of God, the Son of Justice and Truth, the Son of God, in the power of the Spirit that now dwells in us.

In Baptism and Confirmation (and again with Eucharist) we are reminded that our God is here, dwelling among us, within us. Again, from Acts we are reminded that we are not to stand 'looking up at the clouds' expecting to find God up there, but that God is now on earth, among us and our worship and praise is sung and witnessed to in the mighty deeds of God that continue among us. And we must continue to confirm one another in our belief, our worship and our deepening understanding of who we are as the children of God, prophets in the world and bearers of the Good News. We must be aware and be grateful to all the 'Elizabeths' of our lives who validate our faith and bless us, and summon us to publicly declare our prayer in the assembly of believers.

We must ask ourselves if our voices, our words and greetings evoke the power of the Spirit, and if it is the peace of the Risen Lord that is the heart of what we are saying, whenever we meet people. And we must be attuned to all the longings and yearnings of the people of the world, waiting for the fulfilment of God's words, waiting for Jesus' words to come true in their lives, through our belief and practice. We need the community to grow and to mature and to dialogue so that the Word may become reality in the world.

THE BIRTH OF THE WORD MADE FLESH: EUCHARIST

Christ has only one mother in the flesh, but we all bring forth Christ in faith. Every soul receives the Word of God, if only it keeps chaste, remaining pure and free from sin.
Commentary of Saint Ambrose on the Gospel According to Saint Luke

The birth is recorded in one sentence and the child's place on earth in another. 'While they were there, the time came for her to have her child, and she gave birth to her firstborn son. She wrapped him in swaddling clothes and laid him in a manger, because there was no room for them in the inn' (Lk 2:6-7). The actual birth of the Word made flesh is told to shepherds in the field by angels. Now there are many angels and many shepherds, for the Word is spreading into the world. And the whole story is about revealing more about who this child is, what he will do and what it means for all those on earth who seek peace. Now the shepherds will teach Mary and Joseph (the newly initiated) and share their experience of the Word with them.

The shepherds are at work, in the fields, at night, doing what they do in this season of the year. And they are struck with fear at the appearance of glory and the proclamation of great joy. Listen!

The angel said to them, 'Do not be afraid; for behold, I proclaim to you good news of great joy that will be for all the people. For today in the city of David a saviour has been born for you who is Messiah and Lord. And this will be a sign for you: you will find an infant wrapped in swaddling clothes and lying in a manger.' And suddenly there was a multitude of the heavenly host with the angel, praising God and saying: 'Glory to God in the highest and on earth peace to those on whom his favour rests.' (Lk 2:10-14)

The Word is given to the lowly, the poor, the outcast, the shunned, yet those who traditionally have been connected with God's care for his people – shepherds. The child, the Word, belongs to the people and is Messiah and Lord – the fulfilment of all the Jewish hopes and history, and the crucified and risen Lord. This God is wrapped in swaddling clothes (the sign connecting the child to the man who is crucified and buried in a shroud) and lying in a manger, a feeding trough for animals. This child is food for the poor, ordinary food for daily life. This child is the bread (born in Bethlehem) of justice and peace, the bread of hope and salvation. This child is the Word of God – good news of great joy for all the people. This child is Eucharist – thanksgiving and the body and blood of God given to all on earth who seek peace – all those upon whom God's favour and grace rests. These are the same words used to describe Mary, the one yet to hear the good news, prior to Baptism. And this is first communion, first Eucharist, first birth of the Good News, the Word in our flesh. We need others to teach us and give us food for thought, to ponder and come to understand the depth of what is given to us.

The shepherds are sent too, to preach the good news to any and all who will hear and obey the Word of God. And they go in haste to find the child, the Word of joy and peace, which 'the Lord has made known to us' (Lk 2:15). They make known the message they have heard, the song of the angels and all that had been told to them about the child of Joseph and Mary. They preach the good news of God to those newly initiated into the Body of Christ. The word, as the Spirit, goes where it will, to all hearts seeking life and waiting for God's will to be done on earth. And after they have preached to those who have given birth to the Word in their lives, they go out publicly 'glorifying and praising God for all they had heard and seen, just as it had been told to them'. This is the Magnificat psalm being passed on to all who can hear and rejoice along with them. The Word has passed through the believer, just as the people passed through the Red Sea and into the promised land. God gave birth to his people in the power of the Spirit and we are giving birth to the Word in the power of the Spirit and passing onto others what has been given to us. This is Eucharist.

THE BIRTH OF THE WORD IN OUR FLESH

What good is it if Mary gave birth to the son of God fourteen hundred years ago if I do not also give birth to the son of God in my time and culture.
Meister Eckhart

This birth isn't over in a moment. This birth is the beginning of a long labour, a process of bringing the Word to birth in our flesh daily, for all our lives, and sharing it with others, growing in understanding and in the truth of our new lives in God. This is what it means to be Jesus' mother – to hear the Word of God and act on it! Once again, the new believers are confirmed by others – these shepherds who have also heard the Word of God and acted on it. As believers, our individual relationships with God need others in order to grow and mature and deepen. We are told that all who hear are amazed at what the shepherds say. And Mary, the young believer, 'kept all these things, reflecting on them in her heart' (Lk 2:19). This is the second time we are given a description of the effect of the Good News of great joy, the Gospel, on Mary, on us. The word often translated 'treasured', or 'pondered', or 'kept in her heart' is a Greek verb, *rhematos*, which means to store in one's mind for careful consideration, giving careful thought to the words and events and trying to put things together. This word treasured *sun-terreo* and *sum-ballousa* is a complex compound verb that indicates that the message to the shepherds (as the angel's message to Mary) is not immediately perceived and understood. It has to be unpacked and understood in light of her own experience and sifted through her mind, heart and life. This has to be lived with and incorporated into her flesh and bones. There is a lot stirring inside and kicking and seeking expression within.

This idea of each of us who are baptised, confirmed and given Eucharist, giving birth to the Word of God is an ancient experience and teaching. Francis of Assisi writes to his followers:

> We are brothers to Him when we do the will of the Father who is in heaven. We are mothers when we carry Him in our heart and body through a divine love and a pure and sincere conscience and give birth to Him through a holy activity which must shine as an example before others.

THE PRESENTATION OF THE WORD

> Let us rejoice and give thanks, not only that we have become Christians, but that we have become Christ! Do you grasp this? Do you understand the enormous grace God has given us? Stand in awe and rejoice – we have become Christ!
> Saint Augustine

Joseph and Mary obey the law of the Jewish people and give their child to the Lord, presenting him as an offering to God in thanksgiving, and they give the sacrifice of the poor, a pair of turtledoves or two young pigeons. They come to the temple and are met by Simeon who has been sent to see the child, the Word of God made flesh, born into the world. The community of believers grows and each comes to teach the younger members. Simeon is described as 'righteous and devout, awaiting the consolation of Israel' (Lk 2:25), and all that he is, knows and does is bound deeply to the presence of the Holy Spirit in his life.

> … the Holy Spirit was upon him. It had been revealed to him that he would not see death before he had seen the Messiah of the Lord. He came in the Spirit into the temple; and when the parents brought in the child Jesus to perform the custom of the law in regard to him, he took him into his arms and blessed God, saying:
> 'Now, Master, you may let your servant go in peace, according to your word, for my eyes have seen your salvation which you prepared in the sight of all the peoples, a light for revelation to the Gentiles and glory for your people Israel.'

The child's father and mother were amazed at what was said about him; and Simeon blessed them and said to Mary his mother, 'Behold, this child is destined for the fall and rise of many in the house of Israel, and to be a sign that will be contradicted (and you yourself a sword will pierce) so that the thoughts of many hearts might be revealed.' (Lk 2:25-35)

Simeon is steeped in the Spirit and bears the characteristics of a believer who has long since heard the Word of God, pondered it, incorporated it, and lived on it. It kept him alive, hungering for more, for fulfilment and sight of the Word in the flesh of the one he served. And just the sight of the child causes him to break into praise and release, as Elizabeth's voice and blessing caused Mary as a young believer to break into a song of Magnificat about Yahweh, the God of the people. And again, Mary and Joseph are amazed, as they were with the words and responses of the shepherds and are being called to hear again the Word of God through others' voices, faithfulness and experiences. And everything in the Gospel is about the child and who this child is – more than anything one person can absorb or know.

THE SWORD OF THE WORD OF GOD

> You died and were born at the same time. The saving water became for you both a tomb and a mother.
> Cyril of Jerusalem

> The cross is Christ's great sign and trophy of victory.
> Gregory of Palamas

Simeon blesses the young believers, the old passing on the grace of God and knowledge to the younger generation, as Elizabeth confirmed her belief. And he gives words of reality, of what must be faced in the future. Christians were told immediately before their Baptisms that they were already saved, but 'on their knees and under the sign of the cross' (early Christian ritual). And every believer is initiated into the Body of Christ, but it is the tortured, broken, crucified and risen Body of Christ. Whoever this child is, he is God in human flesh, and his words and presence provoke fierce and strong reactions of violence as well as hope. He is the cause of division and persecution for those who will follow him as his friends and disciples. Each believer will be told and taught again and again that, 'if you want to be my disciple, then you must deny your self, pick up your cross and come after me' (Mk 8). And so, young Christians are now confronted with the sword that will pierce their heart so that others' faith will be revealed, tested and found lacking or true. The sword from the earliest day of the Christian community has been the Word of God. Paul tells his community to take up 'the sword of the Spirit, which is the word of God' (Eph 6:17). It is called a two-edged or double-edged sword, cutting to the quick, plunging through flesh, nerve, sinew, deep into the bone and marrow of our lives. It calls us to conversion, to obedience, to put on Christ and to become what we proclaim to be.

But their time in the temple is not ended on such a violent and deadly realistic note. There is another, the prophetess Anna, widowed and elderly, who comes to give thanks to God and who speaks about the child 'to all who are awaiting the redemption of Jerusalem' (Lk 2:38). Total strangers, but believers, are everywhere, in places of worship and in the fields. And they are of all ages, with especially those older in the faith, tried, tested and enduring with grace still. All bring their wisdom and insights, their experience of the Spirit of God to bear upon the younger members of the Church, blessing them and preparing them to be faithful in the future themselves. It is a long labour of becoming the Good News, of giving birth to God in one's own flesh and blood. Again in the words of Meister Eckhart: 'We are all meant to be mothers of God for God is always needing to be born.' Young and old, male and female – all are called to be mothers in this sense.

THE TEMPLE AND THE TOMB

> Lord, who can comprehend even one of your words? We lose more of it than we grasp, like those who drink from a living spring.
> For God's word offers different facets according to the capacity of the listener, and the Lord has portrayed his message in many colours, so that whoever gazes into it can see in it what suits.

Within it God has buried manifold treasures, so that each of us
might grow rich in seeking them out.
Ephrem of Syria

The last portion of the first presentation in the temple ends with a
description of how Jesus grows and becomes strong, filled with wisdom;
and the favour of God is upon him. It could just as easily describe young
believers, who are called to grow in wisdom, holiness, grace and the
practice of their faith over the years, before and after their Baptism,
Confirmation and sharing Eucharist and the Word of the Lord in the
community that initiated them and welcomed them into the Church, the
Body of Christ. The long labour of becoming holy, of becoming Good
News in the world, of being Eucharist, the bread of joy and hope for others,
of being faithful, especially in the face of confrontation, persecution and
the cross, is lifelong.

Now at the end of these two chapters we hear the story of Jesus in
the Temple. He is twelve, the time of a young boy becoming an adult
in the Jewish community, and he travels with his family, relatives and
neighbours/friends to Jerusalem.

But the young man Jesus, the Word of God made flesh, stays behind.
He is fiercely engaged in learning and dialogue, in studying and listening
to the elders speaking of the scriptures and asking questions of them.
Joseph and Mary have returned home, thinking he is with others, and it
is three days before they return and find him in the temple. Everyone who
is listening is amazed, astonished at his understanding and his answers.
These words of description evoke surprise, disbelief, or confusion on
where this information or knowledge came from but, when used in
other areas of the Gospel, it does not usually involve belief or becoming
a follower. And this is the last we see and hear of Mary and Joseph, his
parents; she who has given birth to him and they who care for him. It is
startling and disturbing.

When his parents saw him, they were astonished, and his mother said
to him, 'Son, why have you done this to us? Your father and I have been
looking for you with great anxiety.' And he said to them, 'Why were
you looking for me? Did you not know that I must be in my Father's

house?' But they did not understand what he said to them. He went
down with them and came to Nazareth, and was obedient to them;
and his mother kept all these things in her heart. And Jesus advanced
in wisdom and age and favour before God and man. (Lk 2:48-52)

It has been twelve years, the duration of childhood among the Jewish
people, and the Word has become the flesh of an adult, and he joins his
people and religiously acknowledges God and stands before God in the
temple with the teachers, learning and questioning them himself. He has
come of age. This story is often referred to as the 'losing of the child Jesus',
but it really isn't about losing Jesus, it's about losing one's individualistic,
familial or childish understanding of Jesus the Word made flesh. This is
Jesus, the Word of God in his Father's house, about his Father's business
– the coming of the kingdom of justice, peace, mercy and forgiveness,
which will eventually lead him to the cross and resurrection and his return
to the Father and the Spirit in the Trinity. Joseph and Mary have dwelled
with him for twelve years and it appears they do not really know him at all!

Mary calls him 'son' and he rebukes her and does not respond to her
reminder that she is his mother. He is bound to God the Father in the
power of the Spirit that conceived him. She does not own him, and he
does not belong to her. The relationship of parent, of mother/father in
this world is honoured but it is no longer a primary relationship. And he
is not seen as her son but as the Son of the Father, the Son of God. He
will return with them and he will obey them, but now it is time for her
'to keep all these things in her heart'. What are all these things? Is it all
that has gone before? She has known him twelve years, as he has lived
twelve years. What does she know? Anything? It says clearly that they
do not understand his words. They do not know his heart, who he is and
what he is about. What are all these things? This is the last we see of Mary
as the catechumen, young initiate into the community and believer in
the Gospel. There is no mention of her again as anything other than his
mother, along with his brothers and sisters; she does not enter the inner
circle of Jesus' disciples and friends and he does not go out to her. She
will only be included by name again after Jesus' preaching and life (the
entire Gospel) and his death on the cross and resurrection. She will be
among those gathered when the Spirit comes upon the Church and fills

the community with fire, with boldness, and they are compelled to speak of Jesus Christ, Son of God and Saviour, Risen Lord. And there will be nothing said of her again in the book of the Acts either. She is a follower and a member of the Body of Christ.

Her reaction to Jesus' rebuke of her – that she doesn't know him or understand him and should have known where he would be – leaves her once again being described as 'keeping all these things in her heart' or pondering all these things. This time the word used in Greek is a little different from the previous time. Now these things (*rhemata*) that she treasures are not the word she hears from others but the Word she hears from the Word of God Made Flesh. And the verb 'to treasure' is another form of the verb *terreo-diaterreo* and it means 'to keep something mentally with the implication of duration'. This is a subtle but revealing shift in the verbs and what she is going to do with what she has experienced and what has happened to her. And it is here that the actual Gospel of Luke begins and follows for the next twenty-two chapters. We leave her to ponder all these things in her heart and to begin to hear the Word of God in Jesus who she must learn to follow, and obey. Her primary relation is not mother to son. Jesus' primary relationship is not son to mother. Now she must learn to be a disciple who hears the Word of God and obeys the Word made flesh, putting it into practice in her own life. She must make his words into her flesh and become faithful and true. And this can only be done with a community, with the Church, over a lifetime of 'putting on Christ', and denying oneself and picking up our share of the burden of the Gospel and our cross, letting the double-edged sword of the Word pierce our hearts and lay bare our minds and souls as we die to ourselves so as to live in the freedom of the children of God, and die and rise with Jesus the Risen Lord. This is who we are and what we do. This is how we become Christians in the Body of Christ.

It takes the whole Gospel to incorporate our flesh into the Good News. It takes until forever to begin to understand how, by Baptism, Confirmation and Eucharist, we dwell in the Trinity and relate to God the Father, with Jesus in the power of the Spirit. And we all dwell in the Trinity together, with Jesus praying that one day we will all be one, abiding in God, as God abides as Father, Son and Spirit. We must learn and relearn and be contradicted by the Gospel. We must be challenged to let go of our individualistic or familial understandings of the Word made flesh. We must deal with suffering and death, the cross and resurrection, to know who has taken flesh in our lives and consumes us, converting every ounce of our bodies, souls, minds, hearts and spirits into Good News in the world with others. We are the sons and daughters, the children of the Father. We are conceived by the power of the Spirit and we are the brothers, sisters and mothers of Jesus, the Word made flesh. We must learn this intimacy and passion through hearing the Word of God, obeying the will of God and putting it into practice in our own bodies and lives. This treasuring, pondering, cherishing and keeping all these things in our hearts is the attitude and the position and way of life for a disciple. We are, as individuals and as communities and as Church universal, to watch, to listen, to seek understanding from each other, from all whom the Spirit teaches, to search for meaning in the Gospel and to listen to the words of the Spirit in others, until the Word is born again and again in our flesh and our world. We must live in small communities like the early Church that lived on the Word of the Lord, living through the cycle of readings, the liturgical and sacramental experience of the Paschal Mystery, year after year, initiating others into the Body of Christ, and teaching as we have been taught, yet always learners and always disciples. We must learn to keep losing our limited understanding of who Jesus is and who we are as beloved children and servants of God. We must learn where to look for him in the world – in our Father's house, in the universe, and especially in the Word of God. Our lives after Baptism are forever a *mystogia*, a dwelling ever more deeply in the mystery of the salvation, the mystery of the Body of Christ, the mystery of the Word and the mystery of the Trinity.

We begin the arduous and ordinary task of putting on Christ and being the Word in the world. One of the mystics, Hildegard of Bingen puts this lifelong task into a prayer.

O eternal God, turn us into the arms and hands, the legs and feet of your beloved Son, Jesus. You gave birth to us on earth, to become his living body. Make us worthy to be his limbs, and so worthy to share in his eternal bliss.

The Adult Rite of the Catechumenate

One of my students, Lisa Gerardi, took the understanding of these chapters further and connected the stages of the story of Mary as the new believer with the stages of the RCIA. She writes in her reflection paper: 'The Inquiry or pre-Catechumentate stage is a period of hearing the first preaching of the Gospel. This stage ends with the Rite of Acceptance, a rite where the person making the inquiry states his or her desire to enter the Church to the entire community. Mary says: "Behold I am the handmaid of the Lord. May it be done to me according to your word" (1:38). This is her Rite of Acceptance of her desire to go further in the search for community.' (I told her a good student teaches the teacher!)

The second stage of the Catechumenate can be lengthy, as long as needed by the believer or the group to ask questions, to learn, to become familiar with the sacraments, the teachings of the Church and the Gospel, and to be blessed by the belief and confirmation of others in the Church. This is Elizabeth's encounter with Mary. This stage ends with the Rite of Election and perhaps can be found in Mary's Magnificat and song of the praise of God publicly before the community. Her conversion deepens and depends on others.

The last part of the Catechumenate is called purification and enlightenment. There is still catechetical material and lectionary catechesis, introduction to the scriptures, the gift of the Word of God to the catechumen but the emphasis is on incorporating what one has learned into one's spirit and soul – on reflecting, pondering and beginning to treasure all these things in one's heart. This is usually the six weeks of Lent, though in the early Church it could last as much as three to seven years.

The birth of the child to Mary is the gifting of Eucharist to the believer and the beginning of incorporating the Word of God into the flesh and blood of the community that is to be the Body of Christ in the world. Our lives are living with the Word, as the Spirit takes on our flesh to witness to others in the world. Perhaps we need to think of ourselves as neophytes, novices, beginners for at least twelve years after our Baptisms (even as adults!), remembering that we understand so little about the mystery we have been initiated into. The core of our life begins with the Gospel, the call to conversion by John the Baptist and Jesus beginning to preach in the synagogue of Nazareth, and we must struggle with the Sword of

Truth that is the Word of God, all the way through the Gospel, the cross and resurrection as it lays claim to our lives.

Each of the Gospels is concerned with making new believers. The whole of Mark's Gospel is preparation for Baptism, and a call to return to the community and the Word of God after many have betrayed their faith and given up their practice, in fear. It is Peter who is used as the model of the one who initially follows and then fails, and fails repeatedly. At the Resurrection the young man in the tomb tells the women to go and tell the disciples and Peter the good news of resurrection (cf. Mk 16) reminding the community of Peter's triple betrayal and cursing of the name of Jesus. But he is the model of the one who finally comes to belief and faithfulness, because after the Resurrection and Pentecost he is filled with the Spirit and at the end lays down his life, crucified, but crucified upside down, because he does not feel worthy to die as his Lord died.

In Matthew, it is Joseph in the birth narratives who is seen as the model of the just man, a Jew who learns through the Word of God and the Spirit to break any law that destroys life. This is the model of many in the Jewish community who became believers in Jesus, living beyond the law, into the spirit of the law, and relating to others outside of the Jewish nation. Joseph is the model for the new believer in Matthew's community who lives on faith and who gives his entire life to the service of the child and his mother who could not survive without him. Perhaps we need to work on a catechesis for looking at the conversion and faith life of Joseph as another way of making disciples in the Church today.

From the Gospel of John, we once again, since the renewal of liturgy in the Church of the last fifty years, use the stories of the woman at the well, the man born blind and the raising of Lazarus from the dead when we have catechumens preparing for initiation in the Church, appropriating these stories, as the early Church initially used them to prepare people for Baptism.

And so, in the Gospel of Luke, it makes sense that Luke used the mother of Jesus as the model for the catechumen/believer in his community, seeking to teach the new members of the Church what it meant to become a beloved graced son or daughter of God and give birth to the Word of God in their lives, as part of the Body of Christ sent by the Spirit to witness to the Father in the world.

There is a marvellous Jewish story about the Ba'al Shem Tov who was the founder of the Hassidic movement. A young woman came running up to him one day, desperately pleading for him to pray for her so that she might give birth to a child. She had tried everything, but even after years she and her husband had no child. He said that he didn't have that kind of power, that the power to conceive was in the hands of the Holy One, blessed be his name. The woman begged on her knees and he told her a story.

> Once upon a time there was a woman who wanted a child more than she wanted anything else in the world, and she too went to a rabbi and begged him to intercede for her with the Holy One. She was ignored. But she was not to be put off, and she went home and opened her hope chest that contained what few things of value she owned and treasured. She took out her *katinka*, her wedding shawl, a thing of great beauty, hand loomed and embroidered. It was her most cherished possession. She ran back to the rabbi and gave it to him, telling him to sell it and give it to the poor and then ask God on her behalf for a child. The rabbi took her shawl, knowing its value to her, and told her that God had heard her prayer and she would conceive and bear a child. She rejoiced and danced her way home. And nine months later, a child was born – it was the Ba'al Shem Tov himself!
>
> When the woman heard the story she was excited. She immediately ran home and rummaged through her hope chest and grabbed up her katinka, running back to the Ba'al Shem Tov, shoving it into his hands and saying, here take mine and beg for me a child from the Holy One. But the Ba'al Shem Tov looked at her sadly and said, 'It doesn't work that way. You see, my mother had no story to go by. You must create your own.'

What is marvellous is that we have been given the story, the pattern that makes Christians, by Luke in his first two chapters of the Gospel. In fact we have the blessing of at least four different stories from four communities and four accounts of the Word of God. We have a story to follow and we can creatively and imaginatively weave our own into the pattern of the larger Body of Christ, using the words of the scriptures as the Word takes flesh in our lives. And each of us that gives birth to the Word made flesh in our lives tells another story, brings possibility to others desperate for hope, and is part of the mystery of the Incarnation. The Incarnation takes root in our lives and we live out the Paschal Mystery together, becoming the Body of Christ, practicing resurrection from the moment of our Baptisms, confirming and encouraging and teaching one another with our words and practice. And we break open the Word of the Scripture and feast upon the Word of God, and feast on the Body and Blood of Christ in the Eucharist, as we become the Good News and the bread of peace and justice, the bread of life for all. We are born of water and the Spirit of God, and the Spirit comes upon the Church, sending us out to all the earth, with bold proclamation that we are the beloved children of God, the sons and daughters of the Father, and by the power of the Spirit we are the brothers and sisters and mother of Jesus the Lord. We dwell as one heart, one family in the Trinity! This is what it means to be a true disciple and to belong to the inner circle of Jesus' friends and family. We live now, no longer for ourselves alone but hidden with Christ in God, and we live with Jesus to hear the Word of God and put it into practice in our lives, to act upon it and become what we proclaim by the power of the Spirit – the Good News of God to the poor and all the earth. This is God's invitation to all of us. This is the mystery of our God who from the beginning made us his own, called us very good, and has been trying to make us realise that we are highly favoured and full of grace and that God is always with us, dwelling with us, and that we were born to give birth to God, the Word made flesh in our world. This is the Gospel of the Lord!

There is a closing image that brings us back once again to the last image of Mary that is found in the first chapter of Acts. She is a disciple among disciples, as the Spirit comes upon the Church in fire, that separates into tongues of fire that come to rest upon each person, gathered together. In the monastery of Saint Catherine in the Sinai desert there is an icon of the burning bush of the Exodus account. Moses is drawn to a fire, to a scene that both attracts him and confuses him – a bush that burns, yet is not consumed in the fire. The icon has Mary as the burning bush. And this is how we are to image ourselves as the brothers and sisters and mothers of

God, giving birth to the Word in our worlds, having been overshadowed by the Most High and born of water and the Spirit. Now we are the burning bush, living on fire but not consumed by the Word of the Scripture! We feast on the Word of God and Eucharist and become what we proclaim and believe. We are to live driven by that fire, deep in our bones, consuming our hearts, dwelling now ever more intimately in us. Many of us begin as actual children in our faith and sometimes because of the way we teach our children without drawing them into the community of believers we stay that way – not childlike but without experience or understanding of what we are taught. We must continue to learn as Jesus prays.

> I give praise to you, Father, Lord of heaven and earth, for although you have hidden these things from the wise and the learned you have revealed them to the childlike. Yes, Father, such has been your gracious will. All things have been handed over to me by my Father. No one knows the Son except the Father, and no one knows the Father except the Son and anyone whom the Son wishes to reveal him. (Mt 11:25-27)

We all begin as the children of God, remembering that to be a child in the scriptures is to be among 'the least, the poorest, those without power, except the power of the Spirit'. We must learn the art of being a child of God while growing and maturing in our faith, both belief that we can perhaps articulate but more so practice with others in the Body of Christ. Brother Roger of Taizé reminds his community of this when he speaks: 'A simple prayer, like a soft sighing, like a child's prayer, keeps us alert. Has not God revealed to those who are little, to Christ's poor, what the powerful of this world have so much trouble understanding?'

What if the easiest, the strongest and the most effective way of educating our children is by experiencing the rites of initiation ourselves as adults and then remaining in small communities that feed one another on the Word of the Lord, throughout the liturgical year, celebrating the sacraments together, while including our children at various stages in their development and understanding as the primary way of 'growing in wisdom, age and grace' along with our children? Again early in the Church, the preacher known as the Shepherd of Hermas encouraged his community: 'The great tenderness of the Lord has had mercy on you and your family, and will strengthen you and lay your foundations in his glory. Do not get careless, but take heart and strengthen your family. The righteous word spoken daily prevails over all evil.'

We are not 'wretched' but we are imbued with the grace, the Spirit and the power of God. Our God incarnates in our flesh and dwells with us, finding his home in us, among us and being hope to others through us. Our God in Christ lives at the very core of our reality as persons and as the people of God, living the Word made flesh in us with integrity and passion, and the Grace and Truth of God. Truly together we can all together cry out: 'Our souls magnify the Lord and our spirits rejoice in God our saviour for God has done great things for us and holy, holy, holy is His Name!'

Chapter 8
Cana: Families Facing the World

THE KINGDOM COMES IN THE KITCHEN'S SHADOWS
In John's account of the good news, Mary only appears in two texts: in Cana of Galilee at a wedding feast, and on Calvary, at the cross. The story of the wedding feast is told in Chapter 2, and is followed by the story of Jesus purifying the Temple. The account of the crucifixion (Chapter 19) and Cana are stories that describe Jesus' new order of the Temple, worship, and his community. Mary is present on both occasions though she is not named in either story. These are the only references for Mary and adult disciples of Jesus' family in any of the Gospels. Joseph has died and Mary is a widow.

The story of the wedding at Cana (2:1-11) deals with transformation and radical change set in the context of the institution of marriage. A little later comes the first sign of Jesus' public ministry, the healing of the royal official's son and the transformation of the official and his family into believers (4:46-54). In all Jesus' signs, God's glory is made manifest in the world. The power and extent of this glory grows and deepens as more signs are revealed and as they develop in intensity and power, culminating with the raising of Lazarus from the dead. In addition, each sign marks a shift in Jesus' person and reveals him more fully to the world and history.

The wedding ceremony gathering both families and their friends together as they start out on their own journey reveals that families don't exist solely for themselves but are doorways into the larger realities of extended family and the world at large. Not only are their immediate family and friends invited, but often people who are just connected by work, school, the past and far-ranging connections. The wedding rituals and the feasting afterwards provides a marvellous symbol for what is to come from this couple's union in the future and what their connections to others can become – communion and shared life spiraling out beyond their own small new marriage. This is how the Exhortation describes the spreading out towards others that is mirrored in the first moments of the wedding celebrations. It is found in Chapter 9, 'The Spirituality of Marriage and the Family':

> Led by the Spirit, the family circle is not only open to life by generating it within itself, but also by going forth and spreading life by caring for others and seeking their happiness. This openness finds particular expression in hospitality, which the word of God eloquently encourages: 'Do not neglect to show hospitality to strangers, for thereby some have entertained angels unawares' (Heb 13:2). When a family is welcoming and reaches out to others, especially the poor and the neglected, it is 'a symbol, witness and participant in the Church's motherhood.' Social love, as a reflection of the Trinity, is what truly unifies the spiritual meaning of the family and its mission to others, for it makes present the *kerygma* in all its communal imperatives. The family lives its spirituality precisely by being at one and the same time a domestic Church and a vital cell for transforming the world.[1]

Mary is present at both Cana and Calvary and has a part in the signs. And yet in both narrations her name is not used; instead, she is referred to as 'the mother of Jesus' or, when Jesus addresses her, 'woman' (Jn 2:4, 4:21, 19:25, 20:13). This term 'woman' is one of respect, honour and affection. It singles her out as a member of his larger family – the kingdom where human relationships of blood are not primary. Mary is great because she has been 'born from above' (Jn 3:3-5), and she relates to him as an adult believer, one who works with him and goes before him into the world as a part of his mission. Jesus' movements at Cana set in motion the process that leads ultimately to the cross and Jesus' handing over of his Spirit to the Father on behalf of earth's children. This 'hour' first mentioned at Cana is the 'hour' when the beloved disciple takes her into his care and home at the hour of Jesus' death. At Cana and Calvary the hour of Jesus and the hour of Mary come together. At the beginning and at the end the two are bound intimately together. The story is familiar.

---

1   AL, 324, referencing John Paul II's Apostolic Exhortation *Familiaris Consortio* (22 November 1981), 44: AAS 74 (1982), 136; FC 49: AAS 74 (1982), 141; 'For the social aspects of the family, cf. Pontifical Council for Justice and Peace, *Compendium of the Social Doctrine of the Church*, 248–254'.

Three days later there was a wedding at Cana in Galilee and the mother of Jesus was there. Jesus was also invited to the wedding with his disciples. When all the wine provided for the celebration had been served and they had run out of wine, the mother of Jesus said to him, 'They have no wine.'

Jesus replied, 'Woman, your thoughts are not mine! My hour has not yet come.'

However his mother said to the servants, 'Do whatever he tells you.'

Nearby were six stone water jars meant for the ritual washing as practiced by the Jews; each jar could hold twenty or thirty gallons. Jesus said to the servants, 'Fill the jars with water.' And they filled them to the brim. Then, Jesus said, 'Now draw some out and take it to the steward.'

So they did.

The steward tasted the water that had become wine, without knowing from where it had come; for only the servants who had drawn the water knew. So, he immediately called the bridegroom to tell him, 'Everyone serves the best wine first and when people have drunk enough, he serves that which is ordinary. Instead, you have kept the best wine until the end.'

This miraculous sign was the first, and Jesus performed it at Cana in Galilee. In this way he let his Glory appear and his disciples believed in him. After this, Jesus went down to Capernaum with his mother, his brothers and his disciples; and they stayed there for a few days. (Jn 2:1-12)

In John's Gospel the wedding feast, the place where food is shared, is a privileged place of revelation and a place of worship, liturgy and the preaching of the good news. The gift of faith is shared as surely as the food and drink. The wedding feast is the open door to the kingdom of peace and justice, the entrance used by the Messiah to come into the world. It is the place where the old promises start to come true in surprising ways. Jesus will often refer to wedding feasts and guests, invitations accepted and refused, wedding garments and even who you are seated with when he tells stories about how his new reign/rein/rain of justice and abiding peace for all comes and is recognised in our midst.

The first person mentioned is the mother of Jesus, with the comment that Jesus and his disciples were also present as guests at the wedding. Perhaps Jesus' mother is very aware of unexpected guests, thirteen of them who are enjoying the hospitality and the feasting of the wedding. It is the mother of Jesus who will initiate the fulfilment of the promises and bring forth the hope of the nations and ages. The wedding proceeds and something unexpected happens: they run out of wine. Wine is a rich symbol in Jewish society and in the readings of the prophets as well. The most familiar verse is from Isaiah: 'On this mountain, Yahweh Sabaoth will prepare for all peoples a feast of rich food and choice wines, meat full of marrow, fine wine strained' (Is 25:6). Or in Jeremiah, 'Shouting for joy, they will ascend Zion; they will come streaming to Yahweh's blessings – the grain, the new wine and the oil, the young of the flocks and herds' (Jer 31:12). Wine is gladness, joy, hope, the presence of abundance, justice and the future, promises fulfilled.

And at this wedding feast they have run out of wine! What has held the long waiting of the people together has run out – the time has come for the promises to be filled. The time has come for new wine, new spirit and law, new love and depth of commitment, new expectations and hopes, new life. It begins at this feast.

It is Jesus' mother who makes known the situation and sets in motion Jesus' response. He says to her, sounding to us a bit odd or strange: 'Woman, your thoughts are not mine! My hour has not yet come.' The hour of passion and death, of tearing apart heaven and earth and ripping the Temple's veil in two, and of sundering the distance and separation of divine and human presence has not yet come. Jesus' answer is not easy for us to understand.

Later Jesus has a conversation with his family members that speaks about revealing who he is and what his power can do (cf. Jn 7). The conversation follows the pattern that John uses when people ask Jesus for a favour. First, they must make a statement of belief or show in some manner that they are seeking to believe and follow him. At Cana it seems his mother follows this same testing or growth in her awareness of him and his work in the world. She moves into the kitchen hallways, telling the servants to do whatever Jesus tells them. The die is cast.

Mary tells the servants to obey him. His word is the new law, the new command, the new way of life, the call to conversion and transformation. Obedience to the Word of the Lord brings the kingdom, justice, peace and Spirit into the world.

The word used for servants is *diakonoi*, 'deacons', those who care for the poor, work compassionately in the community, and serve as the living presence of the Word of God in the community's midst. This is the term that John uses consistently to describe believers and disciples. It is the word used for service, for washing feet and for serving at table. It is found in Jesus' description of his true friends: 'Whoever wants to serve me, let him follow me and wherever I am, there shall my servant be also. If anyone serves me, the Father will honour him' (Jn 12:26). It is the term that describes Jesus' relationship to us and to God the Father on our behalf.

These servants are the only ones who know the source of the new wine, made from water, better than the best wine of the old times. They obey the Word of the Lord; they follow his mother's admonitions and exhortations. The water jars, previously used for ceremonial washings, are filled to the brim, and this water becomes the best wine, the true rejoicing and sharing in the Spirit that binds and holds people together. The Law, the Torah, the liturgy and the ritual prescriptions are no longer enough. There is a new order, a new creation, a new spirit and a new liturgy.

This first sign that ushers in the new kingdom eases the burden of a newly married couple; it is an act of compassion and tender regard for their place in the community. It occurs in response to the woman who saw their need, who spoke on their behalf. This is the way the kingdom comes, in response to the need of others, in obedience to the Word. Jesus follows the commands of his mother, who is Church, the new people of God, the new covenant. All the institutions, all the relationships and all the ways of worship, service and obedience must be seen through the lens of this first sign at Cana in the back rooms of the kitchen and hallways with servants and through the eyes of the cross – the hour of glory and radical shifting of all of reality.

The story ends with Jesus going down to Capernaum with his mother and brothers and disciples, who have come to believe in him because of this experience at Cana. We are left, in John's Gospel, with the sense that Jesus' mother (never mentioned by name) accompanies him on his journeys and in his public ministry. She, who brought the Word into the world in her flesh, travels with him and stays with him until the end, until the moment of 'glory' – his passion and death. She is a part of all his choices and actions, by his side always. In John she images an adult family member who is now a disciple in word, in spirit and in the community of believers – what we are all called to be as believers in Jesus.

At Cana, this woman bound to Jesus so tightly has two roles: she makes known to Jesus the needs of the community, and she tells the community, especially those who serve the community, to obey his word. She searches out the needs of people and spends much time in the kitchen and hallways, near the back doors. She herself is servant first and foremost. She knows the needs of the earth and what is needed for life. She knows when freedom, justice, food, hope, housing, medicine, and human dignity have run out and there is no more. She knows that the only way to bring fullness to life, to fill those jars with water, is to do what Jesus tells us. The changing of water to wine, the sign, is prepared for by servants behind the scenes. The kingdom has to do with food, drink, survival and a sense of human worth and dignity within society. It requires a shared passion for justice, for truth, salvation, freedom and life. Jesus' mother is the Church, that woman of compassion, of shared concern, that group of servants who obey the Lord in whatever he says to do.

Families do not exist solely for themselves but exist in concert with other families, in their neighbourhoods, society and the larger world. The fruitfulness of love is found, of course, in the children of the family but it is essential that the family starts early to connect outside their own spaces and relationships with the Church and the world at large. In Chapter 5 of the Exhortation, 'Love Made Fruitful', we read:

> … families are called to make their mark on society, finding other expressions of fruitfulness that in some way prolong the love that sustains them. Christian families should never forget that 'faith does not remove us from the world, but draws us more deeply into it … Each of us, in fact, has a special role in preparing for the coming of God's kingdom in our world.' Families should not see themselves as a refuge from society, but instead go forth from their homes in a spirit of

solidarity with others. In this way, they become a hub for integrating persons into society and a point of contact between the public and private spheres. Married couples should have a clear awareness of their social obligation. With this, their affection does not diminish but is flooded with new light. As the poet says:

> Your hands are my caress,
> The harmony that fills my days.
> I love you because your hands
> Work for justice.
> If I love you, it is because you are
> My love, my companion and my all,
> And on the street, side by side,
> We are much more than just two.[2]

Jesus' family lives in the midst of economic lack and poverty, in an extended family beset with all the problems of being slaves in their own land, occupied by Roman soldiers, with the axis of issues of hunger, starvation, occupation, violence, lack of freedom and the reality of constant threat. They were an ordinary family, like all the others trying to survive and live faithfully as part of the Jewish community. Their daily life was concentrated on the usual work and time devoted to survival but it reflected their belief and devotion to the Torah, to the Law and the Prophets, practiced in public, not only as individuals but more often in community, in concert with others.

We are reminded that families exist for and with others and serve as a model, as a living example of the Kingdom of God in our midst. How families live announces the Good News to the Poor powerfully, in everyday decisions and experiences. Just as Joseph and Mary and Jesus lived as witnesses to their belief as Jews, so do our families today witness in their interactions with others the faith they seek to pass onto their children. Later in Jesus' life, when Joseph had died, he and Mary would

---

2   Ibid.,181, quoting 'Address at the Meeting with Families in Manila' (16 January 2015): AAS
    107 (2015), 178; Mario Benedetti, 'Te Quiero', in *Poemas de otros* (Buenos Aires, 1993), 316:
    'Tus manos son mi caricia/mis acordes cotidianos / te quiero porque tus manos / trabajan por
    la justiciar. / Si te quiero es porque sos / mi amor mi complice y todo / y en la calle codo a codo
    / somos mucho mas que dos.'

have lived what they believed among their neighbours and friends. And it seems it wasn't all that different to any other family. When Jesus begins to preach and teach in public the response of many is 'Is this not the carpenter's son?' (Mt 13:55).

The Exhortation speaks of a married couple's love, but it is the love of each and all of the family members, single parents, widows, those not married, blended families, aunts, uncles and cousins, grandparents/ godparents and friends that become family that witness to the presence of the Kingdom of God in kitchens and on porches and patios, in backyards, back rooms, the street, stores, classrooms, factories and offices, as well as in church and parish. In many countries in Africa, India, Pakistan and the Middle East families are formed from many whose only connection is that they have survived war, invasion, starvation, disease, rape, forced migration and massive destruction. Together they seek to make a family together and to love – to will the good of life for and with one another. This love is called 'to bind the wounds of the outcast, to foster a culture of encounter and to fight for justice. God has given the family the job of "domesticating" the world and helping each person to see fellow human beings as brothers and sisters.'[3]

The chapter goes on to say what this witness and love looks like, quoting from the words of Jesus in the Gospels.

> For their part, open and caring families find a place for the poor and build friendships with those less fortunate than themselves. In their efforts to live according to the Gospel, they are mindful of Jesus' words: 'As you did it to one of the least of these my brethren, you did it to me (Mt 25:40)'. In a very real way, their lives express what is asked of us all: 'When you give a dinner or a banquet, do not invite your friends or your brothers or kinsmen or rich neighbours, lest they also invite you in return, and you be repaid. But when you give a feast, invite the poor, the maimed, the lame, the blind, and you will be blessed' (Lk 14:12-14). You will be blessed! Here is the secret to a happy family.[4]

---

3   Ibid., 183, quoting *Catechesis* (16 September 2015): *L'Osservatore Romano* (17 September 2015), p. 8.
4   Ibid.

Chapter 8: Cana: Families Facing the World   149

All of us as members of our families witness with our lives to what we profess to believe. Our actions, the company we keep, what we spend our incomes on, our priorities as reflected in our time and presence, our engagement in justice for others and our political agendas and who and what we vote for speaks more clearly than anything we say with our lips about our faith. It is learned in our families first. At home and in our daily endeavours is where we 'reflect the beauty of the Gospel and its way of life. Christian marriages [and families] thus enliven society by their witness of fraternity, their social concern, their outspokenness on behalf of the underprivileged, their luminous faith and their active hope. Their fruitfulness expands and in countless ways makes God's love present in society.'[5]

Mary's comments to Jesus at the wedding feast reflect her position in the community not that far from where she still resides, as friend of the bride and groom, and perhaps as a hint to Jesus who has left home and is travelling and preaching, who arrives with an unexpected surfeit of guests – at least twelve – to be mindful of the strain their presence put on an occasion that would be memorable for the couple and the community. She is his mother, but as Jesus refers to her as 'woman' – as we have noted, a title of respect – she is also being regarded as anyone in his new family of those who work with him to uncover the kingdom that is everywhere waiting to be revealed, entered into and lived in with others in radically fresh ways. Anytime and anyplace is now the time and place for new wine and celebrating the presence of God with us with joy.

Our families of origin serve as the foundation of our lives and as the jumping-off point for our way into the larger world. Our families are much larger than just our parents and children. They are inter-generational and include members of our households, in-laws and friends, single persons and other families. As the Exhortation says: 'Friends and other families are part of this larger family as well as communities of families who support one another in their difficulties, their social commitments and their faith.'[6] The document goes on to list what these families within families within smaller communities should provide and who they should seek to connect with and include in their own circle of love and support.

---

5   Ibid., 184.
6   Ibid, 196.

This larger family should provide love and support to teenage mothers, children without parents, single mothers left to raise children, persons with disabilities needing particular affection and closeness, young people struggling with addiction, the unmarried, separated or widowed who are alone, and the elderly and infirm who lack the support of their children. It should embrace 'even those who have made shipwreck of their lives'. This wider family can help make up for the shortcomings of parents, detect and report possible situations in which children suffer violence and even abuse, and provide wholesome love and family stability in cases where parents are incapable of this.[7]

Our families are to resemble the plant described earlier when Mary goes to visit her cousin Elizabeth and her husband Zechariah – hen and chicks including everyone and anyone, especially the least and the most in need in the embracing and comforting shadow of the Spirit that is given to us to share.

There is an old Jewish story called 'Bread in the Ark' that reinforces this sense of Church, liturgy and worship that extends into our kitchen and dining rooms, and out into others' homes and the world at large. It is told in many different countries.

> Once upon a time there was a man by the name of Jacobi. He was a round little man who was going bald – not so much that you'd notice, but a little bit on the top. He was bowlegged and had a bit of a paunch. In fact, Jacobi gave the impression of a round little ball, and people said that the reason Jacobi looked as he did was because of Esperanza.
>
> Esperanza was Jacobi's beloved wife, and she was the best baker in the whole land of Israel. Everything she made was round. She made round pan dulce, round cookies, round cakes, round loaves of bread. Jacobi had a weakness for everything Esperanza made, so he began to look like what she made. The two loved each other dearly. They had been exiled from their beloved Spain, and so they had come to the promised land of Israel and settled there, though they had no relatives or children. Every Sabbath

---

7   Ibid., 197, quoting *Catechesis* (7 October 2015): *L'Osservatore Romano* (8 October 2015), p. 8.

evening you could find Esperanza and Jacobi in the front seat of the synagogue, listening intently to what the rabbi had to say. Now this was very strange, because the rabbi only spoke Hebrew, and Esperanza and Jacobi only spoke Spanish. But they were sure that if they sat there and paid close attention, they would learn whatever they needed for that week to obey God.

One evening Esperanza wasn't with Jacobi. But he was in the front seat, as always, listening with rapt attention to the rabbi's sermon. The rabbi told about a time in the Jewish community in the desert when people cared so much about their neighbours and loved each other so much that they had bread to feed the poor and bread to feed strangers and still had bread left over – so they gave it to God, blessed be his name. On Sabbath evening they gave God twelve loaves of their best white bread, and they rejoiced and celebrated, because they knew that God who is pure spirit doesn't eat bread. But they had bread to waste on God alone.

Now Jacobi didn't get all that. All he got was that God likes good white bread and likes the poor. He couldn't wait to get home and tell Esperanza.

He dragged Esperanza out of her bed and shook her, excitedly telling her about the sermon and the fact that God, blessed be his name, likes bread – good white bread, about twelve loaves. 'And you, you're the best baker in the whole land of Israel. You're going to make God bread and we'll give it to him for the Sabbath.'

That week, Esperanza tried every recipe she could think of in making bread. She tried a little salt here, a bit of cinnamon there, extra butter and lard. She tried different kinds of flour and honey. All week Jacobi ate bread. He ate more bread than he'd ever eaten in his life, but at the end of the week, Esperanza and Jacobi had the best loaves of white bread she'd ever made, twelve of them, to give to God.

Jacobi went early and, before anyone else arrived, hid the twelve loaves of bread, wrapped lovingly in a good white linen cloth, under the seat in front. Then Jacobi listened to the rabbi talk. It seemed to go on and on and on. He couldn't wait for the service to be over. Finally it was done and everyone left. Jacobi looked around to make sure he was alone. Then he walked down the middle aisle toward the ark with the Torah scrolls, and he started talking to God, as Jews sometimes do. 'Señor Dios, have I got a treat for you! My wife, Esperanza, whom you have given to me – blessed be your name – is the best baker in the land of Israel. She has made you a treat.' He opened the doors to the ark and placed the twelve loaves wrapped in the linen cloth inside the ark, along with the scrolls. He closed the doors and hastily went down the aisle. Then he turned around once more and said to God: 'Buen provecho, mi Dios.'

Well, after he left, a weary man came in. He didn't look around but just started talking to God as he walked down the aisle. 'God, I know that you hear the cry of the poor. You tell us in the stories that you care about me and my family. I need a miracle. My family is hungry. I need food. I need to live the way the other people do. I need help. I know that you have a miracle for me. I'm going to read in the Ark of the Covenant where the miracle is.'

He went straight up to the ark and opened the doors. He didn't have long to wait for his miracle – there were twelve loaves of the best white bread he'd ever seen! He stood there and praised God. Twelve loaves! Two for the opening meal of the Sabbath, two for lunch on the Sabbath, two for dinner, and then one for every day of the week ahead. He thought to himself: My family will eat, and I will be able to come and sit with the others and talk of the Law and God when they meet. He gathered up the bread and left.

The next morning Jacobi and Esperanza decided to go to the morning service and see if God liked their bread. As soon as it was over and all had left, they slipped up to the ark and opened the doors. Such love passed between the two of them: God had liked their bread! So, every week for thirty years, Esperanza made the bread, Jacobi brought the bread to God, and the man and his family had bread to eat. Jacobi and Esperanza's love grew, knowing that every week they fed God. Everyone saw how much they loved each other and loved the community they had come to, in exile. The poor man learned a great deal about trust. He learned that if he watched the box, nothing happened, but if he went away and trusted, the bread was always there.

After thirty years Jacobi came into the synagogue before the Sabbath service, as usual. He was a little more bowlegged. He was definitely balder and had a bigger paunch. He was moving a bit more slowly. This time he didn't look around to see if anyone was there. In fact, the old rabbi, who was really old now, was sitting in the back of the synagogue saying his prayers, perhaps dozing a bit.

As Jacobi went down the aisle, he started talking to God as he was wont to do. 'Señor Dios, I have an apology to make to you. The bread is not so good lately, I know, but my dear Esperanza – her hands are not so good. She has arthritis and can't knead the bread the way she used to. Maybe you could talk to the angels and make a miracle. You'd eat better.' He opened the doors to the Ark of the Covenant and put the bread in.

Well, the rabbi jumped up in the back of the synagogue and yelled: 'Jacobi, what do you think you're doing?' He ran down the middle aisle as fast as his spindly legs could carry him.

Jacobi said to the rabbi: 'What do you mean, what am I doing. I'm feeding God his bread.'

The rabbi sputtered out: 'That's the stupidest idea I ever heard! Where did you get it?'

'From you,' Jacobi retorted, 'from one of your sermons!'

The rabbi shook his head and said to him: 'Jacobi, God doesn't eat bread. He's pure spirit.'

'But I've been feeding God bread now for thirty years, every Sabbath.'

The rabbi looked at him sadly and said: 'Jacobi, I can't believe this. Somebody has been stealing your bread. Come, let us wait together and see who it is.'

So the two of them went and hid in the back of the synagogue. They didn't have long to wait. Soon enough, the man walked in, straight down the aisle.

He never looked to see if anyone was there, and he started talking to God as he was used to doing. 'God, I don't want to complain, but your bread – it's not so good lately. It's got lumps in it. I know you feed my family with the bread of angels, but you need to start talking to those angels. They're not paying attention to what they're doing.'

As he opened the door to the ark, the rabbi and Jacobi jumped up and ran down the aisle. They grabbed the poor man by the scruff of the neck, and they all started yelling at each other. All of them felt terrible. The rabbi felt terrible that someone could so misunderstand his sermons. Jacobi felt terrible because something he and Esperanza had been doing for God wasn't for God at all. And the poor man had this terrible feeling that he and his family would never have white bread again.

While they were arguing back and forth, they heard someone at the back of the synagogue laughing at them. It was soft, but it was laughter nonetheless. Who should be standing in the back of the synagogue but Isaac Lauria. Now, in every generation the Jews are given one like Elijah, who prays to God on their behalf and encourages them to wait for the Messiah to come and cares for them. In this generation it was Isaac Lauria. He strode down the aisle and calmed everyone down. Then he said: 'You know who I am.' There were nods of assent. 'You know I talk to God a lot.' More nods. 'And you know he talks to me too.' They nodded again.

'Now,' he said, 'sit down. God has sent me to explain to all of you what happens in this synagogue every Sabbath evening. It is the best show on earth. Every Sabbath evening the Almighty, blessed be his name, gathers together all those who have gone before us in faith, all the angels and spirits of heaven, and especially all the new ones, and they sit and watch what goes on in this synagogue. For this is what makes God's Sabbath holy. Esperanza makes the bread. Jacobi brings the bread to God. The poor man's family has bread. And God gets all the credit! It gives God more joy to see what goes on here in this synagogue with all you crazy people running around than anything else on the face of the earth. But now comes the hard part. Jacobi, Esperanza must still make the bread, and you must still bring the bread to the Sabbath. But you don't give it to God. Instead, after the service, go to the home of the poor man and share the Sabbath meal with his family. You must still believe with all your heart and soul that this gives God more pleasure and more joy than anything else on the face of the earth.'

So it was. And so it is still. For God's sake, whatever we want to do for God, we must do for the poor now. The new order of worship, of life shared together, has begun. Now, each of us as individual disciples and believers, in our marriages and families, in our parishes and public lives, in the Church, must live as the 'woman' Mary the disciple and widow who knows the needs of the community, reminds us to do this now for her Son and to do it for those in need of compassion and help, food and dignity and acceptance in the community. Now it is our turn to keep walking back and forth between the front rooms and the kitchens, our homes and others in the neighbourhood, and in cities and countries to share one another's common needs and live together as the children of God. So it was, and so it is today and will be in God's kingdom among us.

Chapter 9
The World Family: The Cross

SHADOW OF MERCY

In John's Gospel, the second text that includes the mother of Jesus deals with the last words of Jesus as he dies and hands over his Spirit to the world in the Church (cf. Jn 19). The chapter begins with Pilate having Jesus scourged. The soldiers crown him with thorns and mock him, and Pilate questions Jesus about who he is and the nature of power. Then, in the name of Caesar, he gives the order to have him crucified. The actual description of what happens to Jesus is just two lines: 'Bearing his own cross, Jesus went out of the city to what is called the Place of the Skull, in Hebrew: Golgotha. There he was crucified and with him two others, one on either side, and Jesus was in the middle' (Jn 19:17-18).

There are five scenes in this narrative of Jesus' passion and death: Jesus crucified between two others, with the description of who Jesus is – the Nazorean, King of the Jews; the throwing of dice and the tunic of Jesus not divided; the women at the foot of the cross; Jesus thirsting; and the body of Jesus pierced by the lance, with blood and water flowing from his side. These five pieces of the story talk about Jesus' kingdom coming and the characteristics of Jesus' new creation, new family and liturgy that has come into the world.

Juan Alfaro, OSB, says that the five marks of the Church are indicated by these scenes: universality (from the Hebrew, Latin and Greek languages on the notice that said who this person was); unity, from the fact that Jesus' tunic was not divided; maternity, from the presence of his mother at the foot of the cross (all believers and followers have the same mother, the woman); spirituality, because only the waters of Spirit quench Jesus' thirst; and sacramentality, specifically Baptism and Eucharist, which are born from the side of Jesus in water and blood.[1]

The woman Mary, the one in the middle, the heart of the five marks, is the mother who stands near the cross. This nearness to the place of

---

1 See his *Mary, Woman-Mother of Christians in the Struggles for Liberation in the Gospel of St John* (San Antonio: Mexican American Cultural Center, 1979).

suffering and injustice is her place, the place where obedience at last brings her, as it brought Jesus himself. She stands with others: a sister named of Jesus' mother – Mary, wife of Cleophas, Mary of Magdala, and the beloved disciple, who is never named in the Gospel – because it is everyone ever baptised into the Community of the Beloved Disciples, John's church. Jesus sees her there and calls her 'Woman'. He tells John, 'Here is your mother'. The woman is herself a disciple, and both mother to the disciples and mother of the community itself, the Church. This woman still is nearby. She stands in solidarity, and she still is given to all disciples beloved of God. She gives birth to the Word in us and attends us, especially in suffering and death. We are meant to become this mother, as we are to become the beloved disciple – for one another within the community and in witness together for others. Where we stand with others in the world is more witness than any of our words.

This 'seeing', this noting of the presence of someone, is an important thread in John's Gospel and it is emphasised by the repetition of the word 'behold'. The NAB translation reads, 'Woman, behold your son', which connects with 'Behold the lamb of God' (Jn 1:29) and Pilate's 'Behold the man' (Jn 19:5). These words reveal a new reality, a new relationship and a new truth that will bind together this new people of the covenant. Mary is now not only his mother, but she is handed over to his followers, his last gift to them.

The disciple took her into his home. This describes anyone who accepts the Word of God and the will of God with faith (cf. Jn 1:11-12, 3:11, 5:43). To accept the Word is to accept the mother, the new relationships in community, and the new order of worship, communion, unity, universality, reconciliation, thirst for the Spirit and liturgy. Mary, mother and disciple, is one of the firstborn of this new community on Calvary. Jesus gives birth to her in his hour as he gives birth to all believers; he makes her Mother of the Church.

The woman is the symbol of the new people, the poor, those living in hope of liberation and freedom, those singing with a prophet's passion for justice and right ordering of the world's people and structures. For John, the mother of Jesus is a person who believes and calls others to obey the Word. She knows the needs of all the people of God and presents them to her Son, yet she also knows it is obedience to the Word that sets the changes in motion. She accompanies him on his journey and ministry and is with him from the beginning of his public work to his death and the beginning of the Church, its birth from the side of Jesus' body.

At the cross she becomes mother of all Christ's disciples, and they learn from her, just as he did and we do, the meaning of poverty, humility, obedience, reverence and mercy. She is given over to the Church, the first gift after the Spirit, to his own brothers and sisters, to survive with grace and faithfulness.

In Central American countries and in countries of Africa, Asia and the Middle East it is primarily the women who, against the law, go out into the fields and search the highways and dumping grounds for the bodies of their loved ones. They hound the jailers and courageously walk into danger to find their loved ones, often only to bury their dead and give them dignity at least in death. In many Latin American countries there is a tradition, celebrated on Good Friday evening after all the services are done and a light meal taken. The women gather again at the cross, and they retrace their steps and retell the stories again of the presence of God and how he died. They walk the Stations of the Cross backward, remembering all that happened and singing and praying, keening and crying. Then they go home.

There is also the tradition of the *pésame*, the remembering of the passion of Jesus and the sorrow of his mother. *Pésame* is an expression of condolence, of saying 'I'm sorry for your loss', of extending, even to strangers, a gesture of compassion and concern, seeking to ease their pain and to be with them in their grief. The *pésame* is celebrated in early evening on Good Friday, after the sorrowful mother has been witness to the death of her child. All come back to the church to console the Virgin, the woman of sorrow, to be with her as she remembers, as she stands in silence near the shrouded body of her dead child. There are devotions and prayers, songs and meditative silence. The people are there to share in her sorrows and to share their own sorrows with her. The reality of brutality, of unnecessary suffering and death, of injustice and inequality is shared together.

The *pésame* takes the form of a statue (or a woman who represents the grieving mother), dressed in funeral black and standing first at the foot of the cross and then at the head of the coffin as the corpse is taken

down from the cross. The weight of the wood, the weight of her grief and
tears is shared with all believers, and we are allowed to share our sorrows
with one another. As mother of the executed criminal and as a woman
struggling to believe in her son's message, she had to deal with anger at
the people who failed him and forsook him in his hour of need. She had
to deal with those who murdered him and the fear of his friends. She
had to forgive them all. The presence of Mary at the *pésame* is a reminder
to the people that Christ was not completely abandoned at his death;
there was one willing to pay the price with him, to stand beside him in
his agony. It is this solidarity with Christ that makes Mary our mother
and our model. Her presence at the cross reminds us that to identify and
struggle with those who are broken and outcast and alien is to take upon
ourselves their own inhuman conditions. It is to live with the shadow of
the sword of truth and justice.

The shadow of the cross is long. The old are abused. Women
and children are beaten. There is violence in the streets and in our
neighbourhoods; poverty, insecurity, lost jobs, under-employment;
raising grandchildren; single-parent families; drugs and alcohol; ugly
divorces. There is anger, rage, slaps and screams within families and
relationships. For some, crimes and jail are a part of family life. There
are gangs, and children for whom no one takes responsibility; the old
and sick and weak no one claims. And all this is just on a personal and
family level.

The shadow of the cross is in the death penalty, abortion and the push
for physician-assisted suicide – euthanasia. And there are the larger human
abuses of greed, insensitivity, nationalism, racism, classism, violence,
war and the build-up of weapons, the displacement of whole peoples
and the slaughter of communities. Around the world there are massive
problems confronting the survival of human beings, not only individuals
and families but whole cities and countries due to forced migration. The
earth, ground, air, water, all that has been created along with human beings
are in danger and struggling against these evils. There are many places to
stand now at the foot of the cross with the three women and the unnamed
disciple. Just the single issue of forced migration screams at us, with all
the issues of injustice that accompany those on the way: food, water,
sanitary conditions, clothing and shelter, continued medicine and health

care, education, safety and help in dealing with trauma and what they have known in relocation and settlement – often in foreign countries with different languages, religions and customs, along with the coping with loss of everything familiar and loved. *Amoris Laetitia* singles it out because of the numbers it involves in every country of the world.

> Human mobility, which corresponds to the natural historical movement of peoples, can prove to be a genuine enrichment for both families that migrate and countries that welcome them. Furthermore, forced migration of families, resulting from situations of war, persecution, poverty and injustice, and marked by the vicissitudes of a journey that often puts lives at risk, traumatises people and destabilises families. In accompanying migrants, the Church needs a specific pastoral programme addressed not only to families that migrate but also to those family members who remain behind.
> … Migration is particularly dramatic and devastating to families and individuals when it takes place illegally and is supported by international networks of human trafficking. This is equally true when it involves women or unaccompanied children who are forced to endure long periods of time in temporary facilities and refugee camps, where it is impossible to start a process of integration …[2]

All these victims are entrusted not only to Mary, the woman, the mother, but she stands with the Beloved Disciple and the others that belong to John's Community of Beloved Disciples, and so they are entrusted to all of us. She stands with them, silently sharing and bearing their suffering as her own. If we want the consolation of our mother and if we want to console her in her sorrow, then we must comfort all her children. With Mary we must forgive and bury our rage and bitterness at friends, family, relatives, neighbours and all others. We must give birth with her and her Son to courage, to heartfelt hope in one another and in this new community. We must allow the Spirit to give birth in us to the world's families – the family of nations, of all we share this earth with as brothers and sisters. This image of Mary is given to encourage us to become mothers and fathers to the

---

2   AL, 46, referring to *Relatio Finalis* (2015), 23; and Message for World Day of Migrants and Refugees on 17 January 2016 (12 September 2015): *L'Osservatore Romano* (2 October 2015), p. 8.

outcasts and all those the world sees as 'expendable', worthless and treat without dignity or even a shred of basic human kindness.

This is the new world, where there is crucifixion but also connections, communion and consolation. We are given a mother, Jesus' mother, but we are given more: Jesus' father, who provided for him and his wife for countless years; a community, a family, brothers and sisters; friends of God – bound together in shared grief, pain, anger and forgiveness as we give birth to the Word of God in the world and God as our Father. At the foot of the cross we sing together Mary's Magnificat and see clearly which side we are on. Where the Virgin of Sorrows is, the Man of Sorrows is. We also give witness to the silent and mysteriously quiet man who fathered Jesus in the world, Joseph. It is where the children of God, the friends of God are found. Are we there?

One of the phrases prayed and sung in the *pésame* service is: 'Come all you who pass by the way, look and see whether there is any suffering like my suffering?' (Lam 1:12). In our pain we look for Jesus, and find Mary and one another near the cross. Together we are given hope and courage. At the cross, with Mary, we pray and take sides. In shared pain we are given courage. In shared grief we are given hope. In shared anger and horror we are given forgiveness and mercy. No one must suffer alone. It is called Good Friday. It is good that our God has gone through all of this with us, stays with us, gives us his mother and his community of beloved disciples and friends, and his father, Joseph, and our Father Abba. We can go home together and believe that new life and resurrection will come. We can go home and wait for the dawn to come. We can go home together and sleep gratefully, believing steadfastly in resurrection.

But we must remember that the 'woman' stands with others: three others. 'Meanwhile, standing near the cross of Jesus were his mother, and his mother's sister, Mary the wife of Clopas, and Mary Magdalene. When Jesus saw his mother and the disciple whom he loved standing beside her, he said to his mother, "Woman, here is your son." Then he said to the disciple, "Here is your mother." And from that hour the disciple took her into his own home' (Jn 19:25-27).

Three of those standing in solidarity and communion are women and the other is the unnamed disciple who is everyone baptised into John's community – their new relationship as the beloved disciple of Jesus. Two are members of Jesus' extended family by blood and marriage who are part of the Community of Beloved Disciples. The other two are part of Jesus' family by grace and favour, by the power of the Spirit. And the words given to the one 'whom Jesus loved' have strong echoes of Joseph, the father of Jesus who does not fear 'to take her into his own home'. All of us in the family of Jesus are summoned to stand at the foot of the cross with all those who are bound in the water ties of Baptism and the Spirit and in the blood ties of shared survival, suffering and death. The Father of Jesus was there, as was his father on earth, along with all those who have gone before us in faith and those who stand with us now until forever at the foot of the cross of the world, bringing together our love of God, stretching up towards Our Father and our love of one another stretching outwards to encompass all the rest of our family, all the brothers and sisters and mothers and fathers of God.

A friend of mine, Rob Young, OFM, wrote a story for Holy Week for the Native Americans of the US Southwest with whom he lived and sought to serve. It is called 'The Song of the Mountains'. It reminds us of the nature of this new community born in the shadow of death.

Once upon a time there was a people that lived far off, away from all others. They were sometimes called the people of the Mountain Spirit. They lived simply and often very poorly. As time went on the villages were attacked by a terrible pestilence. The disease came first for their children, then for the old, and then for the strong. Soon they realised that if something wasn't done it would destroy all the people.

So the elders gathered and brought together all the strong ones left in the villages. One of the elders spoke: 'The ancient wisdom tells us that the Mountain Spirit protects us. He has always protected us and sent us rain and shadows when we needed him. He has always nurtured us. It is time for us to use the ancient wisdom. We must choose one of you to go to the mountain and beg the Mountain Spirit to save the people.'

One of the strong asked: 'What must we do to beg the Mountain Spirit's blessing?'

One of the old ones answered: 'There are only two things you must do. When you travel to the mountain you can take with you only what you need in order to survive the journey, and you must give what is left of that as gift to the Mountain Spirit in exchange for the song that you are to bring back from the mountain and sing to us.'

They talked all night, and finally one young man said: 'We must run to the mountain across the great desert lands. All that I need, all that the people need, in order to survive such a journey is water. I will take water with me as a gift to give the Mountain Spirit in exchange for a song of healing and protection.'

They agreed that this one would go on behalf of the people – he had the gift for the journey.

He rested the remainder of that night and then got a large skein of water. He left before dawn and began to run across the desert. He left full of expectation and hope that he would save his people. As the day wore on he grew tired and thirsty. The sun was hot and harsh. He took only small sips to keep him running.

He had been out more than six hours and it was almost noon when he met a young woman and her child coming toward him dragging sacks of cactus fruit they had harvested from the desert. They were weary and tired. The woman stopped him and pleaded for a little bit of his water for her child. He thought to himself: I am strong, and she is tired and her child is in need. I can spare a little of the water. The next few times I want to drink I won't. There will be enough. And so he shared his water with them.

He ran on, through most of the afternoon. Late in the afternoon he came across a small patch of shade in the desert, a lone tree. Underneath it lay an old man in its shade, patiently waiting to sing his song and welcome death. The young man stopped beside him and greeted him, and the old man asked for a bit of water. So the young man knelt before him and gave him some water, so that he would be able to sing and greet the Great Spirit with fresh voice and soul. Then he ran on with the rest of his precious water.

Finally, as the shadows lengthened, he came to the base of the mountain and was ready to climb. By nightfall he would be able to pray to the Mountain Spirit on behalf of his people. But as he started to climb, he heard the sound of moaning, of pain. He glanced over and saw a coyote caught in a trap. Now coyote was a trickster, but sometimes coyote was the Great Spirit. One never knew. He went over to the trapped creature, set him free and washed his wound with water and wet his tongue, and the coyote limped off.

Then the man started to climb the mountain. He climbed, and as darkness fell he brought out his water skein once more to offer his gift to the Mountain Spirit. And he realised with dismay that he had no more water. It was all gone, the last little bit had evaporated in the heat. He was broken-hearted. He had failed his people. Without a gift the Mountain Spirit would give no song and the people would continue to die. He had failed the elders who had entrusted him with this mission of mercy.

As he thought about his failure, the winds came up strong, blowing from many directions. A storm was coming. He crawled onto a ledge and into some rocks and waited for the storm to pass him by. All he could think about was the deaths among his people: the old, the children, and even his own friends who were strong had died from the fever.

He began to weep and keen and howl in grief. His voice rose loud and bounced off the walls of stone around him. Then the rain came, hard and driving. The tears ran down his face and mixed with the rains from the sky, and he couldn't tell the difference between his pain and what seemed to be the mountain's fury. Finally, the storm abated. He sat quietly afterward, full of peace and yet sad. He knew he had to go back to his people without the song.

And so, during the long night, he ran again across the desert. When the dawn came he arrived back at the edge of his village. The elders were waiting for him on the edge of the village, along with all those who could walk or drag themselves out. The young man fell on his knees before them and confessed that he had failed them, that he had run out of water by the time he got to the mountain. The elders looked at one another and knew that he had been their last hope. The people would die.

As he knelt on the ground, he began to cry and weep again for his failure and for the death and suffering of his people. He rocked back and forth and lifted his arms to the skies and mourned with cries and groans that all the people recognised as their own death cry. But just as the storm had come in over the mountain, now the storm came again, racing across the desert floor, with howling wind and swirling dust. Once again tears ran from the young man's eyes and the rains came pouring down so that the sky's tears mixed with the man's tears. His tears and the rain moistened the earth and when his tears were done and the rains were over they came from the village – the old and weak, the children, the sick – and they were healed and whole again.

There was rejoicing all day, feasting and dancing, singing and drumming. Late that night the elders gathered again and the young man joined them.

'I do not understand,' he said. 'I had no gift to give the Mountain Spirit, and so I did not receive the song. Still, the people are healed. Why are we saved?'

An old grandmother spoke after long silence: 'You were to bring with you only what you needed for your journey and to give that to the Mountain Spirit as a gift. The only thing you needed in order to survive you gave. It wasn't the water. It was compassion for your people. The Mountain Spirit took your gift and gave you the song, the song of suffering and the song of sorrow shared. And so the people will live.'

If you travel across the desert of the Southwest in Arizona there may be rain and storms that come up quickly. And if you sit very quietly in the dark of the desert's night, you may hear the Mountain Spirit's song on the wind, and all the people will pick up the chant and sing the song. It is the song of compassion. But it could be any desert in Africa, the Middle East, Asia, anywhere in the Arctic wilderness of the far north, anywhere on our earth becoming more parched and dried out.

Mary, along with the others at the foot of the cross, tells us this is where we stand: where all the ones who mother and father us in our faith and lives, the men and women, the beloved disciples, the friends of God are to be found everywhere in the world. This is where the Church is to be found everywhere. As Blessed Oscar Romero reminded all his families and parishes, his Church: 'A Church that does not join the poor in order to speak out from the side of the poor against the injustices

committed against them is not the true Church of Jesus Christ.' We will
be remembered for where we stood and whose cross we sought to carry,
and then to stand with them in their suffering and death, if we could not
stop the injustice and evil that claimed them. We are to be remembered
for our gift to God: the love of our people and our compassion for them,
for one another, for all. This saves us, this song of suffering we learn near
the cross of God's child Jesus. Together each of us and our families and
friends, God's friends are to sing this song for all God's beloved children.
Together we will grieve and wait together for the resurrection.

Prayer of Grieving
Mary and Joseph, remember us in our sorrow. You once lost the child
Jesus who was given into your care and searched frantically for him,
never understanding the reason for his disappearance. You found
him, but would lose him again, taken from you in death, brutally
and violently. But Jesus disappeared into the grasp and hand of God!
Pray with us and grieve with us who also have lost 'the apple of our
eye'. Help us to remember that they are in the grasp of God and that
God is holding onto them with his tender and strong love. Give us
the courage to live, to not grow bitter but grow in compassion and
justice for all those who are vulnerable and need protection. Comfort
us and make us a place of sanctuary in this world, and to live with
grace until we are all come home again in God. Amen.

OUR LADY OF GUADALUPE
As noted, there are uncountable traditions and devotions regarding Mary
throughout history and found in every culture. Each of them has a shadow,
a singular understanding of who Mary might be, about her child, the Word
of God made flesh among us, and about Joseph, whether he is specifically
mentioned or not immediately apparent, such as the ones that concentrate
primarily on the relationship of Child and mother. One of these devotions
is found in the Latin American and Indigenous Nations theology and
history of the Americas (which has also found its way across oceans,
connecting to believers in all the other continents), that of Our Lady of
Guadalupe. Joseph is not mentioned, reflecting the historical reality of
conquest, enslavement, destruction of families, impoverishment, rape

and slaughter of the Indigenous people. (Devotions surrounding Joseph, however, are found in the theologies of labour and workers, liberation, the land and farmers, and in all Indigenous cultures.) To that end, I offer the story of Our Lady of Guadalupe for an understanding of how devotions can be connected to the Scriptures and to the Holy Family of the Trinity.

John the Baptist of the Americas

Long, long ago, in 1531, in the bridge that connects North America to South America, a civilization lay in ruins. Its people had been conquered by an invading army, their culture destroyed, cities razed, women and children raped, brutalised and murdered, enslaved, and their religion and gods thrown down. They were devastated by people claiming to be Christians, children of the true God. In that ravaged land, where the Indian population had shrunk because of disease, despair and slavery, a man, a simple peasant who had been baptised into the new religion of Christianity, was on his way to Mass one morning. In his mid-forties, he was walking on the outskirts of what is now Mexico City.

It was before dawn, cold, a Saturday, the day after the feast of the Immaculate Conception. As he walked he heard music. It started out with just the birds, then it seemed as if the earth began to sing underneath his feet and in all the bushes and brush around him. And then a light came out of the ground, spreading to the skies. It seemed to shimmer and move, like a fountain, and suddenly on the path in front of him, with her feet planted firmly on the ground – her bare feet – was a young woman. She was beautiful and, like him, an Indian, one of the indigenous people of the broken and shattered land. She spoke to him in his language, Náhuatl, and asked, 'My son, Juan Diego, where are you going?'

'To Mass at Tlatelolco.'

She spoke to him again: 'You must know and be very certain in your heart, my son, that I am truly the ever-virgin Mary, holy mother of the true God, through whom everything lives, the Creator and Master of heaven and earth. I wish and intensely desire that in this place a church be built. Here I will make known and show forth my love, my compassion, my help and my protection to the people. I am your merciful mother, the mother of all of you who live united in this land, and of all peoples, of all those who love me, of those who cry out to me and seek me and of those who have confidence in me. Here I will hear their weeping, their sorrow, and will remedy and alleviate their suffering and misfortunes. You must go and make known my intentions to the bishop of Mexico. Tell him that I sent you to him, and that it is my desire to have a sanctuary built here.'

Juan Diego looked at her entranced, overcome with joy, and then hastened to obey her.

He went quickly to the house of Bishop Zumárraga after Mass and joined the long line of beggars, visitors and delegations waiting to see the bishop. When he was finally ushered into the bishop's presence, he poured out the story of the lovely lady on the hill of Tepayac outside the city. The bishop merely told him to come back at a more convenient time, and sadly Juan Diego started back home.

The lady was waiting for him, as sunset came over the land, just where he had seen her at dawn. He was embarrassed and told her that she should send someone else to the bishop. And he told her that he was sorry that he had failed and saddened her heart. But the lady told him to go back the next day.

So, the next day he was back in the long line of beggars waiting to see the bishop. After a long day in the sun, he was ushered in. He told the bishop that the woman was Indian like him, and the mother of the true God – and his mother too – and that she wanted the bishop to build her a church on that ground.

The bishop listened to the story but didn't believe him for a moment. He told Juan Diego, 'Go back to your lady and tell her I want a sign that confirms who she is before I do anything.'

That night on the path the lady was waiting for Juan Diego again. After listening to him, she told him to come again in the morning and she would give him the sign.

But Juan Diego returned home to find his Uncle Bernardino very ill. All day, on Monday, 11 December, he took care of his uncle and did not return to the lady on the hillside. The next morning, on 12 December, he hastened again to the city, avoiding the hill of Tepayac and the lady. But she was waiting for him on the other side of the hill and asked him once again where he was going. He poured out his heart to her, about his uncle and his concern.

She spoke to him: 'Listen, my dear child, and know that I will protect you. Do not let your heart be dismayed. Am I not here? I am your mother. Is not my help a refuge? Am I not of your kind? Do not fear for your uncle, I will take care of him. In fact, he is already better. Is there anything else that you need?'

Then she told him to climb the hill and that he would find flowers blooming. He was to pick them and bring them back. The hill was scrub, cactus, weeds, thistles and thorns. But Juan Diego found roses, Castilian roses, wet with dew, with thick, strong scent. He came back to the woman with his arms full of flowers. She took the roses and arranged them lovingly in his *tilma* (a cloak made of hemp fiber), wrapping him and the roses together, and sent him off to the bishop.

Again Juan Diego waited long in line. Finally, he was allowed into the bishop's study. He stammered out that the lady had sent him again, with the sign. He opened his cloak, and the roses cascaded out onto the floor in front of the bishop. Then the bishop fell on his knees, because on the *tilma* was a picture of what Juan Diego saw – the woman of light standing on the earth, the woman Mary, the mother of the true God, *la morenita* – and he realised that Juan Diego had truly seen the mother of God on the road outside the city. All that night Juan Diego and the bishop talked, but there is no record of their conversation.

Within ten days the first small chapel was built of adobe, and the bishop left the city to go to the hill of Tepayac, where the cathedral and shrine of Our Lady of Guadalupe now stand. Six years later nine million Aztec people had been baptised as Christians. Our Lady of Guadalupe had become the bridge between those conquering and those who were destroyed. She is the patroness of the Americas. We are all her children, and she is with us when we suffer and need comfort and solace. But she still is found only on the roads outside the city, outside the centres of power and domination and wealth. She stays with the poor, those who are still conquered and excluded from the centres of society and religion. Whenever we see her, she wants us to go to the existing powers and tell them that she wants them to change.

She is called Our Lady of Guadalupe, *Nuestra Señora la Virgen de Guadalupe*. Perhaps the 'of Guadalupe' is because the Spanish people listening couldn't understand what Juan Diego was saying to them. An Aztec Indian, like the lady, he was speaking in a language new to them: Náhuatl. There is a place in Spain called Guadalupe, where there had been devotion to Mary for decades before this appearance. But Mary did not speak the language of those who came with cross and sword: Spanish. She spoke the language of the oppressed, the slaves and indigenous whom many in the Church believed had no souls. The translators heard it and associated it with the place of devotion in Spain. But there are many translators who say that the word in Náhuatl is closer to a word that means source of hidden underground waters. So the lady was given a name by the conquerors from the other side of the waters, yet she stands firmly, geographically bound to the conquered, the slaves and the poor. She is one of them, aligned with them in race, language, sorrow and desire.

This is a strange, disquieting story. The young woman says she is the mother of the true God and our mother, the mother of all children united in this land, all races, all men and women, the mother of all the oppressed, the slave, and the lost, as well as the mother of the conquerors. She only reveals herself in relation to her children, beginning with her firstborn son, Jesus, the crucified and risen One. She is persistent in her choice of a messenger, insisting that the bishop must bend to her wishes by listening to one without status or power. She wants the bishop to know the truth. In sending an Indian and making herself one with them, she is quietly telling the bishop that he and those with him are wrong. It is now time to do what should be done for these people, her own beloved children.

There are many visions and appearances of Mary, but none these days that deals with power and taking down the mighty from their thrones and raising up the lowly in their place. It is a strong vision of Mary that alters power structures and resists evil. She demands that those in authority, especially those with religious authority, know the truth and reverse their decisions, their lifestyles and choices, to change and to stop what they are doing in collusion with others in her child's name. She wants them to deal with wrong, with sin and evil, and she will not go to them herself but sends one of their victims to speak in her place. She makes them come to her, outside their base of power.

In such situations as appearances, we have a tendency to regard the appearance itself as the remarkable thing. With Our Lady of Guadalupe, it is the effects that are astounding. Why does she appear to the least, to the peasants, the poor, the crushed ones of history, to the Indians of Mexico instead of to those who come with the Gospel, the light of salvation and civilization? More than four hundred and fifty years ago she came, barefoot, as one on pilgrimage to a holy place. She picked a hill, ground holy to the Aztecs, the place of Tonantzin, who was venerated as the mother of the gods, the source of life and one who gave hope and direction to their lives, who could take the form of either man or woman. She came to the 'liberators' and to the martyred and murdered and massacred, trying to hold all of them together in her encompassing care. She made it clear that some of her children were to be challenged and some of them were to be consoled; building a sanctuary of remembrance and a gathering place for the new people was necessary. This new life, new birth, new people and new promise was a gift from her and her child to those whose former life and temples and culture were destroyed. A new era, a new civilization and a new people were born on Tepayac. The powerless, the poor children of God were sent and missioned to the powerful and told to evangelise them, to call them to renewal and reconciliation. Mary set foot on that bridge, that land mass between two continents, North and South America, the place that symbolises where the many races, cultures, languages, economies and policies have met, clashed and joined.

What does this appearance say to people? Does it say that the poor are more worthy of Mary's care? Yes, it does. Mary is poor, and so she has a special affinity for the poor of the earth. God became poor in the flesh and blood of Jesus. God came as a poor child in an occupied territory and died poorer than anyone could ever have dreamed.

The majority of the people in the world are poor. The new statistics from the United Nations and other NGOs state that North Americans, who are less than 5 per cent of the world's population, use 68 to 82 per cent of the world's available resources. That leaves the remaining 95 per cent of the world's people surviving and struggling with what's left. One of the new definitions of what constitutes being rich is this: if you have more than what you need in order to survive today, then you are rich, because the majority of the world's peoples do not. The world economies, lands and natural resources are deteriorating steadily. This is true even in portions and areas of the United States: Native American reservations, border regions, inner cities, rural areas. Archbishop Dom Helder Camara of Brazil says that people can live in poverty, but they cannot live in misery, worse than animals.

So Mary comes to this land and reminds us vividly of those who need the most attention and care: the weak, the sick, the elderly, the cast-offs, the babies and women, the broken and the bent, those afflicted and impoverished by others. Mary is mother to all, and she cares most for those who share her experience of poverty, misery, human suffering and injustice. She lived in poverty, in the midst of violence, when political intrigues swallowed whole peoples without concern, under the shadow of slaughter and oppression. When Mary appears, it is to remind us that devotion to her is dangerous to any existing form of power or structure or individuals that treat other human beings as worthless, expendable, or as enemy. She appears in history to remind Christians that those who call themselves her children must be brothers and sisters to all her children.

If we believe in Mary and her child, then we must care about her children who are still being rejected, crucified, tortured, broken by power, disappeared, raped and defiled.

The place she picked to stand on, the ground of the hill Tepayac, announces the place of hope, of life, and of the universe, for it was there that the indigenous people worshiped the gods and goddesses of earth, plants, water, sun, moon, stars and all growth. It is much like a kiva –an underground cave in the US Southwest where the Indians still dance and do the rituals of becoming, recreating, renewing and coming of age.

With her feet planted firmly on the ground, Mary says to take care not to destroy the earth, let alone the people connected to these holy places. She warns us to be careful that the way we practice our religion is in balance with the world, that we live in harmony and peace. Our place is to honour the poor and the indigenous people of every country. Mary always sides with the lost and forsaken, whether in Mexico City of old, or more recently with the Muslim women in Bosnia, the slaughtered in Rwanda, the victims of the Sendero in Peru, those dying of cholera in Syria and Yem, and those starving to death while the world watches. The litany is long and universal across this earth. These are her children. Where she appears must stop being a killing field, a battleground, a scorched earth, a scene of inhumanity among her children. Mary is consolation, mercy and protection for those most in sorrow and in need of care – abandoned by the world to God alone. Like God, who bends to hear the cry of the poor, Mary bends before God and before her children suffering and dying at the hands of others who call themselves her children too.

How did Mary look at Tepayac? For those who understand the symbols of the Náhuatl and the Aztec nation, she is an icon, a story picture, much like a stained-glass window. She is a living and breathing hieroglyphic of colour, detail, design and form, who reveals without even speaking a wealth of meaning. She stands flat on the earth, barefoot, a young Aztec girl, fondly referred to as *la Morenita*, 'little dark one'. She is one of a race of men and women who were destroyed, their land and goods confiscated, with nothing left to hold onto – not even life itself. The few chronicles and poems left from this era reveal nothing but the futility and desperation of their lives under the Spaniards, without hope or recourse. She is brown-skinned, as opposed to the 'white' Spaniards.

Her face is visible, unveiled. In the Aztec religion the gods and goddesses are masked, distanced from those who revere them. But she is approachable, familiar. Her face is one of compassion; the window of her soul is inviting, full of care and tender regard. She is the one who knows of and has great concern for the ill, those sick unto death, trapped in circumstances of misery and hunger, lacking necessities, weeping in sorrow and despair, helpless in their plight. The depth of her caring shows in her face.

Her eyes are looking downward – reverent, humble, saying she is not one of the gods but a human, like us. Her hands are folded in the traditional manner of the Indian offering a gift or herself in service to another. She is offering Juan Diego her help, protection and solace, and she is offering all the people her love and mercy and power with God. Her hands are just above her heart, pointing outward and upward, offering comfort and herself in humble service. Enlarged photographs of her right eye reveal three figures, one who appears to be Juan Diego, the second Bishop Zumárraga, and the third, his translator Juan González. Her face is joyous and serene.

She is clothed in blues and greens – turquoise, deep blues, the colours of waters and skies. The colours are sacred to the Aztec, signifying harmony, peace, contentment and the reconciliation of opposites. She wears a belt, a sash wrapped high above her waist. The black cincture, visible just below her hands, appears in the Aztec fashion of one announcing pregnancy. Since she is pregnant, then, to see Mary is to see Jesus who dwells within her. He is hidden in an oppressed people waiting to be born. He gives them sanctuary, sharing his own mother with them as foretaste of the life to come. It is Mary who bears Jesus and therefore faith in him to the people of Mexico. It is clear from this birth of Jesus among the Aztecs that the new age, the new life of the people, is to come.

Part of the design in her dress is the colour of dried blood, for she alone knows the depth and extent of her people's pain and suffering. Her face seems to change; sometimes she looks very Indian, and at other times she looks more Anglo, as though in her own flesh she has drawn together the diverse peoples of the land.

The name Guadalupe, more fondly Lupe, means 'hidden river'. To a people used to living in a barren and arid land, water is crucial to survival – to quench thirst and produce food. Because of her, a dry hill produces roses, glorious rich red vibrant roses, a sign of celebration, joy, simple happiness. Along with the heavenly music heard by Juan Diego, the hidden waters and the roses proclaim *fiesta*, the time and place of shared hope and delight along the way. She is *niña mia*, 'my little girl', to Juan Diego, a little one, a child of the same God to whom he now belongs. She is also mother to this God, as well as mother to all God's children. She is justice to her children and mercy to the victims of injustice.

After much study and examination, it is thought that the angel and the cloud below her, the sun rays at her back, the stars on her mantle, as well as the gold borders on her clothes, have all been added to the original painting on the *tilma*.

It is interesting that the hemp fibers of a *tilma* usually disintegrate within twenty years. It has been over four hundred and fifty years and the image of Our Lady of Guadalupe is still vibrant.

The hope Mary extends to her people is not one projected dream-like into the future but is promised now, even in the midst of their suffering. She offers the hope of resurrection for a people, a nation who had learned to see only death. She gives the people a reason to live again, a faith in the future that transforms even the death of their own civilization. She proclaims that God saves history through the power of the poor. She has become the patroness of land reform movements, revolutions of the poor and the peasants, the protectress of the farm workers. She reclaims the land for God. And because her only request is that a sanctuary be built where those in need can come for solace, she also reclaims the land for the people.

She is Advent personified; like John the Baptist she goes before the One who is coming. Let us listen to the Word of the Lord from the second Sunday of Advent:

> This is the beginning of the Good News of Jesus Christ, the Son of God. This beginning had been foretold in the book of Isaiah, the prophet. 'I am sending my messenger ahead of you to prepare your way. Let the people hear the voice calling in the desert: Prepare the way of the Lord, level his paths.' (Mk 1:1-3)

Mary, like John, is the voice from the wilderness saying no more war, make peace among enemies, lay down arms and pick up pruning hooks, and make your swords into plowshares so that even the lion and the lamb might lie down together. The voice in the wilderness is the cry of the poor, and God hears that voice always, though others often seem deaf to its cry. If this is true, then repentance is in order. This is preparation for what is coming: good news for the poor, the binding of broken hearts, the proclamation of liberty to captives, freedom to those languishing in prison, the announcement of God's favour and the day of vengeance, comfort to all those who mourn, a garland instead of ashes, the oil of gladness instead of mourning, a garment of praise instead of despair (cf. Is 61:1-4).

Mary, like John, is a witness, alert, speaking the truth. This word of Isaiah that John echoes continues further on in the chapter: 'I rejoice greatly in Yahweh, my soul exults for joy in my God, for he has clothed me in the garments of his salvation, he has covered me with the robe of his righteousness' (Is 61:10-11). In another translation, this last description is 'the mantle of justice'. In the tradition of the prophets, Guadalupe heralds God in heavenly song and in the faces of the poor, the wayfarers, those on the way, on the roads outside the cities, in the deserts. She is the hidden underground river, the source of joy that comes in human form among us.

She calls us to repent, to care for the ill, the weak, the poor, the slaves, the displaced and dispossessed. She wants us to do the works of justice now, immediately, before her child comes among us and stays forever among the outcast and unwanted. She and John echo the same traditions and beliefs. In her, the children of God are waiting to be born, looking for a place that welcomes them on earth, a community that cares for them. She, with John the Baptist, lives between the Old and the New Testaments, the Old and the New Worlds, the continents. She is a bridge strung across suffering to hope, this resting place of roses and spring in winter, of joy in the midst of despair, of poverty shared. She speaks words of tenderness and healing, of peace to come, and of the promise of her presence, along with her child, to those in need and pain.

Mary is both the dark one and the light, the candle burning more and more brightly, the light coming from within, the fire gathered that will burst forth in the midst of darkness. She is the strongest and most enduring prophet of Advent, the woman of hope. She is ready and waiting for all of us, the watch woman at the gate, the first to see, to say yes and to open to the Word, the presence of God in human flesh, borrowed from her own bones and soul. She goes before the face of the Lord to bring to her people knowledge of salvation and forgiveness of their sins. She comes with the rising sun, as a work of mercy, shining on those who live in darkness and in the shadow of death, guiding our feet into the ways of peace (cf. Lk 1:76-79). She proclaims that the fullness of time is close, waiting to bloom in our midst unexpectedly, as a child, as peace with justice, as hope enfleshed in the corporal works of mercy, as the kindness of God bending down to earth to sing to us, as a mother sings to her baby about to be born.

Guadalupe is the embodiment geographically and historically of what incarnation means in this continent of the Americas and what must

happen if the promises of justice and peace and community are to be born
and grow among the many nations and peoples of this land, especially
along borders. *Nuestra Señora la Virgen de Guadalupe* is John the Baptist for
that continent and its peoples. Her cry is of care for the poor, repentance
for injustice and invasion, and restoration of dignity and hope among her
children. It is the fundamental imperative of the Gospel of her child, and
she announces the message clearly by siding with those who reveal the
face of God hidden in our midst today.

This woman is wrapped in a mantle of justice, clothed in the robe of
her people's suffering. She is the prophet who goes before the coming
of the Sun of Justice, responsible for her children's needs and intent on
calling her wayward children home to justice and peace, calling them to
be responsible for all her children.

This is a story from the continent of the Americas. Mary, under
many titles and names, is the patron and protectress of many countries
around the world. And so is Joseph. He is the patron of Canada along
with workers, day labourers, fathers. Every country and region of the
world sees, perceives and reveals the persons of the Holy Family: Joseph,
Mary and Jesus as belonging to and like them in appearance, language,
culture, tradition, sharing their reality in their history. Whether it is
Mary, the Mother of Palestine watching over all the diverse children of
God in the land where Joseph, Mary and Jesus lived so long ago, or the
Woman of Africa, or the Joseph of countries in Eastern and Western
Europe or a man and a woman in traditional Asian dress, in an Inuit
village or New York city: Joseph, Mary and Jesus are universal symbols of
holy families everywhere. Each representation of this father, this mother
and this child reveal something of the mystery of the Holy Family: our
Father, the Beloved Child and Spirit of the Risen Lord. And so, every
member of every family also reveals and conceals some aspect of the
mystery of our God in whose image we are made: The Trinity. We are
all made in this image and likeness of God and we best and more fully
reveal our God when we live in communion, in family, in the Body
of Christ, in all the world – we are all shadows of the Family of God.

In the closing chapter of the Exhortation, 'The Spirituality of Marriage
and the Family', we find this reminder from the scriptures: 'Each of us,
by our love and care, leaves a mark on the lives of other; with Paul, we

can say: "You are our letter of recommendation, written on your hearts … not with ink, but with the Spirit of the living God" (2 Cor 3:2-3).[3]

There is a story told by many people; I first heard it from a sister in Africa, Maureen Cahill, in a mission clinic in Northern Transvaal. It is called 'The Parable of the Pencil'.

> There are a number of things to remember about a pencil. First, all the goodness or true worth lies within. Everything is within us – the power of the Spirit, the presence of the Word listened to and absorbed, and even The Child, The Word to be born in our flesh.
>
> Second, a pencil needs to be sharpened as it is used. As we go through life, we are 'used up'. The traces and shadows of The Spirit, of the Word and our Father that we leave behind grow shorter or longer, but we are always casting them.
>
> Third, the whole reason for a pencil's existence is to leave a mark. Each of us alone and within our families and in the world say with our presence, our words and actions and in our relationships that X marks the spot where others can find our God. Now because of the Incarnation – God taking hold of our flesh and dwelling within and among all of us announces that now the privileged place, the dwelling place of God in the world is in every human being
>
> And fourth, a pencil is always in someone else's hand. All of us write love letters to the world from God. Others teach us how to hold the pencil, how to form letters and in many ways how to write, but we are always in the hand of God who holds us dear.

Guadalupe, the mother of the only true God, the God of justice and mercy, is like a pencil, and we, her children, are to follow in her footsteps, pointing the way home. Like mother, like daughter. Like mother, like son. Jesus was entrusted to Joseph and Mary as the place of entrance into the human race and history. Now every family is an entrance way into the presence of our God, a place for God to be welcomed and to dwell among us. In Chapter 5 of *Amoris Laetitia*, we read these words:

---

3 AL, 322.

By their witness as well as their words, families speak to others of Jesus. They pass on the faith, they arouse a desire for God and they reflect the beauty of the Gospel and its way of life. Christian marriages thus enliven society by their witness of fraternity, their social concern, their outspokenness on behalf of the underprivileged, their luminous faith and their active hope. Their fruitfulness expands and in countless ways makes God's love present in society.[4]

Every family is a holy family. There is always something new to say about our God. There is always another way to express what our God looks like – every family is a place of revelation that both conceals and reveals this fathomless mystery of The Family we are born into and are called to be a part of, with all families as God seeks to make us all one in The Trinity. Whether we are in Ireland or Israel and Palestine; in Libya, China, Peru, India, Kenya, Greece, the islands of the Pacific, or the Arctic, in Mexico, Italy, Russia or the United States – in every city or tiny village there is a family that is a trace of the Holy Family, The Trinity.

---

4 Ibid., 184.

Chapter 10
The Shadows of Grief and the Shadows of Resurrection

Somewhere, something incredible is waiting to be known.
Carl Sagan

When death claimed the child of Joseph and Mary, Mary went home, probably with those who with her mourned his terrible death. They were all Jews and so, even in their grief, they would have gone home, perhaps back to the Upper Room where they had celebrated just evenings before and celebrated once again the ritual of the Sabbath. This weekly ritual began with a woman lighting the candles and singing the blessing that welcomed the Shekinah, the Spirit of God that had gone into exile freely with the people until the Messiah would come. The Shekinah stayed with the people during Sabbath and left when the week began again. The Sabbath preparations would have fulfilled the old ways, in obedience to the covenant, affirming the promises of the past, the scriptures and the prophets. Like all Jews she would have gathered together with her friends, relatives and neighbours to praise the God of history, no matter their own personal loss. They would listen to the ancient words. They would have pondered together the burden of seeking to understand and accept, to bend to the will of the Spirit, and to believe in the God who suffered with the people, heard their cry in slavery and led them at last into the promised land flowing with milk and honey. They would have listened to the old stories – the promises of the Suffering Servant of Yahweh, the promises of peace with justice for all, and the coming of new wine and the oil of gladness to be poured out upon the people who would stream to the city of Zion.

After the prayers and meal the day would be silent, a time of rest, prayer and reflection. They would be numb with grief, trying to internalise the cross, the execution – its brutality and senselessness – and the fact of death, loss and emptiness. Jesus' life was stopped, and a piece of her soul and their lives was stopped forever. They would be exhausted with weeping, their hearts and even their bodies pulled to that body, aching in physical solidarity, part of them in the tomb. They would eat because it was expected and sleep only through exhaustion. They would go on living, dragging themselves through the long night and day.

In her heart and the heart of all the beloved disciples and friends of Jesus they would bear the pain, the sense of injustice, of rage, of bitter sorrow and death, chewing on it like she had chewed on all the words and events since she was first pregnant and bearing such good news in her womb, sharing it with Joseph who accompanied her. She would remember and pray and be preyed upon, knowing the sword within her soul, digging deeper into her heart. She would see and know others for what they were, revealed in the harsh glare of death, looking around her and seeing those whose hearts were true and breaking along with her own.

They endured, and waited for the dawn to come, for the Sabbath to be done, so that they could go to the tomb. There was nothing else to do.

Did she spend the day alone? We do not even know if she was in Jerusalem for the feast, or whether she was still in Nazareth. Did the women – her relatives and the other women who tended to the Master's need – seek her out? The other side of faithfulness is endurance, witness and martyrdom, the handing over of our own lives, dreams and hopes until there is nothing left to give. Yet, who is to say that this does not contribute to resurrection, to the mystery of the will and the ways of God.

She might have made shrouds or wrapped herself in them as good Jews wrapped themselves in prayer shawls, remembering how she had once wrapped her newborn in swaddling cloths. She would have remembered all the innocents murdered, all those who died while waiting for the vindication of Jerusalem and the coming of the Messiah, all those who had been faithful and martyred in the long history of her people. There were so many. She would have joined the long line of those who looked at life in the teeth of death, the day after death claimed a piece of their heart and soul.

But, we believe resurrection comes! Earth itself knows first, the stone rolled away, the tomb burst open, and the ground spitting forth what it could not contain. The tombs had opened and the Temple veil had split in the storm that had accompanied Jesus' death. But this resurrection took place in silence, the silence of the darkest part of the night before the sun starts to move across the earth, when shadows start to lengthen in the light. She would have waited for the dawn of the daystar, as she and all Jesus' followers and friends did, learning in their flesh and in history the consequences of saying yes to God. It was and is, perhaps, the last lesson all of us learn before resurrection shatters all of creation and the vision comes true in flesh shining with glory and declaring peace and blessing for all.

We know her experience and those of the first believers that pondered the words of Jesus:

> Truly, I say to you, you will weep and mourn while the world rejoices. You will be sorrowful, but your sorrow will turn to joy. A woman in childbirth is in distress because the time is at hand. But after the child is born, she no longer remembers her suffering because of such great joy: a human is born into the world. (Jn 16:20-21)

This distress is part of what brings forth resurrection. This endurance and faithfulness is necessary for life to take hold again where death has once held fast. This is love put to the test, love that survives death itself and learns another way to express itself. We all must face the shadows of death, suffering, grief and the emptying out of our hearts. It must be done by each of us and all of us together. This is the way Dorothy Day, the founder of the Catholic Worker, writes of these feelings and sense of dying before we die that enters our lives over and over again.

> One of the greatest evils of the day among those outside the proximity of the suffering poor is their sense of futility. Young people say, 'What good can one person do? What is the sense of our small effort?' They cannot see that we must lay one brick at a time, take one step at a time; we can be responsible only for the action of the present moment but we can beg for an increase of love in our hearts that will vitalise and transform all our individual actions, and know that God will take them and multiply them, as Jesus multiplied the loaves and fishes.
>
> The greatest challenge of the day is: how to bring about a revolution of the heart, a revolution which has to start with each one of us. When we being to take the lowest place, to wash the feet of others, to love

our brothers with that burning love, that passion, which led to the cross, then we can truly say, 'Now I have begun.'[1]

Or to put it in one line: 'You love out loud even when it seems you have nothing to offer.' This line is from Malissa Winkowski in a post while she was digitising Miss Day's work over the years with the Catholic Worker in New York City.

We do not only face these moments alone, but we face them in our families and among our friends. Resurrection begins in the very first moments of our lives and takes on an even stronger character and power in Baptism. It is confirmed and celebrated with thanksgiving in countless moments throughout our lives. God our Father raised Jesus from the dead in the power of the Spirit, and Jesus, who was torn and stretched in life and death by the extremes of compassion and violence, is more alive and present and more powerful among us than when he lived for three short decades on earth, sharing our flesh and mortality in the mystery of the Incarnation. And we stake our lives on this reality and believe fervently that one day God our Father will raise us with Jesus in the power of the Spirit and we will know a fullness of life that is shared with the Risen Lord.

But this mystery and way of living that we call resurrection life has been seeded in us and we live our lives moment to moment in this freshness and power of life radically altered and deepened, practicing the art of resurrection in the face of all that happens in our lives and world, in our histories and geographies today. We call it grace, the favour we have found with God, the Spirit of the Risen Lord, breathing in us, abiding in us, transforming us, clothing us with the power from on high, wrapping us as though in an invisible cloak of life and light hidden in our bodies and souls now.

Our bodies are frail and mortal and yet we carry resurrection within us. God became one of us and shared his power and authority with us, sending us forth to be his presence of Good News to all the earth. Part of the mystery of the Resurrection is not only did God as our Father raise Jesus, his beloved Child, freeing him from death by the breath of the Spirit but he raised him up to face down and liberate us all. Jesus was a Jew, born in and living as a slave in his own land, oppressed and poor, living on the edge of life, among those just struggling to survive. He came

---

1   Dorothy Day, *Loaves and Fishes: The Inspiring Story of the Catholic Worker Movement* (New York: Harper & Row, 1963).

from the bottom and died on the outskirts of Jerusalem, where refuse and garbage was thrown. Resurrection is seeded and found in all the places in our world today that know such despair and devaluation. They are found all around us, in our families and work places, cities, rural areas, churches and countries. Where are we looking for this vibrant altered life within life to emerge? Are we aware of it hidden in so many faces and families so close to us? This is what resurrection, found even now in our frail bodies and tentative stands against the forces of death, looks like today.

This declaration and proclamation of belief comes in contemporary form. The following is from writings constituting a community called 'Public Theology Reimagined', which is sponsored by an online forum called 'On Being'.

> The scars in Jesus' hands, feet and side expose the brutality of the Roman Empire and every other empire that seeks to crushed the most vulnerable through social, political, or economic degradation. The baptised community of Jesus is most whole when, instead of mocking the frailty and vulnerability of others, we embrace them. The body of Christ is frail. It is scarred. It is flawed and beautiful and this is good news.
>
> The task of this era is to be more open about the unique ways in which we've all been wounded by sexism, homophobia, racism, ableism and other theological barriers to flourishing. We are invited to voice a bold 'No' to every force and practice that would diminish our unique and collective resemblance to God. 'No' to impulses that lead to isolationism, Islamophobia and irrational fear. 'No' to the mocking of disabled reporters and persons. 'No' to laws and policies that target and brutalize lesbian, gay, bisexual, transgender and queer people. This 'No' emerges from the same soil in which we find God's 'Yes' in Christ. The 'Yes' that sees people as beloved creatures, not lifeless cogs in the wheels of unrestrained capitalism and militarism. The 'Yes' of God that dignifies Jesus' trauma on the cross and our traumas in everyday life through courageous remembrance, not cowardly erasure. And that is the threat of moral authority: that the frail yet risen body of Jesus is a living antagonisation of the powers that be.[2]

---

2 This piece was written by Broderick Greer and is entitled: 'Frail Bodies Are a Witness to Resilience and Resurrection' (Easter, 2017).

This is core to what all of us and our families are facing in contemporary society worldwide. Chapter 2, 'The Experience and Challenges of Families', in *Amoris Laetitia* tries to detail many of these and other issues that impact and destabilise every kind of family on so many levels. 'The strength of the family "lies in its capacity to love and to teach how to love. For all a family's problems, it can always grow, beginning with love."'[3]

The end of this chapter of *Amoris Laetitia* reminds us of where we stand today and how to face the future together in our families and as the family of the Body of Christ and the human family.

> The Synod's reflections show us that there is no stereotype of the ideal family, but rather a challenging mosaic made up of many different realities, with all their joys, hopes and problems. The situations that concern us are challenges. We should not be trapped into wasting our energy in doleful laments, but rather seek new forms of missionary creativity. In every situation that presents itself, 'the Church is conscious of the need to offer a word of truth and hope ... The great values of marriage and the Christian family correspond to a yearning that is part and parcel of human existence.' If we see any number of problems, these should be, as the Bishops of Colombia have said, a summons to 'revive our hope and to make it the source of prophetic visions, transformative actions and creative forms of charity.'[4]

Decades ago, around 1979, I travelled to Pueblo, Mexico, and for a short while lived with an extended family in a sprawling garbage dump on the outskirts of the city. Their father had died when a building he was working on had collapsed. The mother was in her early forties. In the lean-to shacks constructed of pieces of cardboard, tin and tarp, along with anything else that had been salvaged in their daily searches through the dump, there lived at least twelve to fifteen people, sharing what they had. There were two grandfathers, one related to them, the other having been taken in. I had been told that there were others; at least three brothers had left to try to make their way in the city, begging and doing odd jobs. They had been about thirteen years old when they left, telling their mother that there

---

3   AL, 41, quoting *Relatio Finalis* (2015), 10.
4   Ibid., 57, quoting *Relatio Synodi* (2014), 11; Colombian Bishops' Conference, A *tiempos difíciles, colombianos nuevos* (13 February 2003), 3.

would be more food to share with the others and that they'd try to bring something back whenever they could. At least five of the children were abandoned 'strays', having lost parents and needing a family and a home.

Into this fold I was welcomed, and treated with warmth and graciousness.

One evening, as the sun was starting to go down behind the hills of refuse, Maria, the designated mother/parent, and I walked along one of the high paths on the top of the garbage. There was still many there, sorting and picking through the trash, looking to see what they could salvage, recycle and use themselves. The stench was awful, though after a week or so I was getting somewhat used to it. I finally asked her: Maria, how do you do it? How do you get up every day and face this, facing into every evening exhausted, listening to the rumblings of the others' stomachs, sensing their bodies tossing and squirming on their mats while they try to find troubled sleep?

She was quiet for a while, and then she answered me. Her response stunned me and reduced me to tears. She simply said: I believe in the Resurrection. We live on a garbage heap, like where Jesus died, and one day we will be set free and we will know what it is to live. He is with us. He liked being with all of us who are on the bottom of the pile. She looked at me and smiled, saying teasingly: I think you'd call it liberation. We have been saved and lifted up. He's right here with us. Every morning when I get up I pray that I'll see him walking towards me sometime today. She paused for a second and then added: and I always do.

I have never recovered from that profession of faith. And in those short weeks, I learned what a family really is.

In Chapter 3 of *Amoris Laetitia*, 'Looking to Jesus: The Vocation of the Family', we find these quoted words:

'The covenant of love and fidelity lived by the Holy Family of Nazareth illuminates the principle which gives shape to every family, and enables it better to face the vicissitudes of life and history. On this basis, every family, despite its weaknesses, can become a light in the darkness of the world. "Nazareth teaches us the meaning of family life, its loving communion, its simple and austere beauty, its sacred and inviolable character. May it teach how sweet and irreplaceable is its training, how fundamental and incomparable its role in the social order." (Paul VI, *Address in Nazareth*, 5 January 1964).[5]

Nazareth is not only a place in the Middle East today, the place where the Holy Family settled after returning from exile and running in fear from all that sought to cut short their lives. Nazareth, as well as every holy family, is a relationship, singular and diverse, graceful reality that can be found and created through life-giving love and human community anywhere. As Maria proclaimed her faith, we all must learn that resurrection life too is everywhere in every situation and in every family's life, no matter its failures, its oddities and strangeness or its way of living.

I was struck by Maria sharing with me how she would pray every morning upon awakening. Years later I discovered an ancient hymn by Symeon the New Theologian called 'We Awaken in Christ's Body'. I now associate this hymn with Maria Elena and often remember it when I awake, no matter where I am – home alone or staying with families around the world.

We Awaken in Christ's Body
We awaken in Christ's body
As Christ awakens our bodies,
And my poor hand is Christ, He enters
My foot, and in infinitely me.
I move my hand, and wonderfully
My hand becomes Christ, becomes all of Him
(for God is indivisibly
Whole, seamless in His Godhood).
I move my foot, and at once
He appears like a flash of lightning.
Do my words seem blasphemous? Then
Open your heart to Him
And let yourself receive the one
Who is opening to you so deeply.
For if we genuinely love Him,
We wake up inside Christ's body

---

5   Ibid., 66, quoting *Relatio Finalis* (2015), 38.

Where all our body, all over,
every most hidden part of it,
is realised in joy as Him,
and He makes us, utterly, real,
and everything that is hurt, harsh, shameful,
maimed, ugly, irreparably
damaged, is in Him transformed
and recognised as whole, as lovely,
and radiant in His light
he awakens as the Beloved in every last part of our body.

What we believe and experience in our bodies we also believe and experience in our relationships, in our families and with our friends – with all our beloved brothers and sisters of Jesus, the Child of God. Together in the power of their Spirit we call God Father in the family of which we are all invited to become a part – the family of the Trinity, our God who is Three and yet One. We are all born for love. And all of us, regardless of our family situations, make-up and configurations, are made to one day know the communion that is one family: The Trinity. For now we are shadows of that Holy Family, but shadows of light, of truth, of grace and favour that remind us that we who know the mysteries of the Incarnation and the Resurrection in our bodies and our families are already a part of that Holy Family that holds us all with such tender strength and inclusive, wild and unbelievable grace-filled life. We are all holy families already.